Graveyard Empire

GRAVEYARD EMPIRE

FOUR DECADES OF WARS AND INTERVENTION IN AFGHANISTAN

BY EMRAN FEROZ
TRANSLATED BY ADAM BALTNER

OLIVE
BRANCH
PRESS

An imprint of Interlink Publishing Group, Inc.
Northampton, Massachusetts

First published in 2024 by

Olive Branch Press
An imprint of Interlink Publishing Group, Inc.
46 Crosby Street, Northampton, MA 01060
www.interlinkbooks.com

Originally published in German as *Der längste Krieg: 20 Jahre War on Terror*
by Westend Verlag, 2021

Cover art by Harrison Williams

Library of Congress Cataloging-in-Publication data available
ISBN-13: 978-1-62371-106-1

Printed and bound in the United States of America

For Maamaa Waheed

Contents

Introduction

WHEN I WAS writing the final lines of the German version of this book in May 2021, the situation in Afghanistan was changing hourly. The Republican Afghan army and other various pro-government militias were losing their ground while the Taliban were conquering one province after the other. It seemed that the whole so-called peace process, a term that the US administration also pushed, was a myth. The intra-Afghan dialogue, which many Afghans hoped for, was dead. Thanks to the Doha deal signed around one year prior, the Taliban created new realities. They considered themselves the winners of America's longest war and the slayers of another empire that invaded Afghanistan. On August 15, 2021, the first Taliban forces entered Kabul. A few moments before, Ashraf Ghani, the country's Western-installed president, fled the country together with his corrupt aides. Kabul had fallen, or in the words of the Taliban; it was liberated. Once again, different narratives played an important role in Afghanistan's history. In 1992, the mujahideen rebels conquered Kabul, then ruled by Soviet-backed dictator Mohammad Najibullah, in a similarly triumphant way and called it "Fatha"— liberation, as the Taliban do today. However, there were several major differences between 1992 and 2021. When the mujahideen entered Kabul, Najibullah was in his third year of rule after the fall of the Iron Curtain and the withdrawal of Soviet forces from Afghanistan. After a decade-long occupation, the Red Army faced a harsh defeat, but policymakers in Moscow decided to continue to support what they had built over the years. After the withdrawal, Najibullah's regime received financial and logistical support. Also, to some extent at least, ideological beliefs remained either. Throughout the decades, large cadres of the Afghan Communists were ideologically brainwashed by Moscow and, like their opponents who fought for Allah, became staunch believers in their cause. Three decades later, it could not have been more different. The Western-backed Afghan Republic mainly consisted of deeply corrupt politicians and brutal warlords who maintained their mafia-style networks to enrich themselves through billions of aid money or military contracts with NATO troops. The Afghan parliament, often described as a Western achievement of democracy by apologists of the ruling kleptocracy, turned into a bazaar of corruption and immorality in its early stage while many rural sites were haunted by CIA-backed death squads and Predator drones—all of which led to some of the most gruesome impacts of the US-led War on Terror in Afghanistan and ultimately to the rebirth of the Taliban.

For most Afghans, Washington's twenty-year intervention was simply a continuation of the wars and conflicts that had ravaged their country since the 1970s. At that time, however, armed struggle in Afghanistan had attracted little interest. Many people in Western states had been mostly or completely ignorant of the country. To many ears, its very name had an exotic and mystical ring, evoking something of the unknown. Perhaps a few had heard of the Hindu Kush mountain range, and how throughout history many different empires had invaded this region (or even that a war was supposedly happening there). Still, Afghanistan had nothing to do with their own lives. All this suddenly changed on September 11, 2001, when nineteen terrorists attacked the World Trade Center in New York and the Pentagon in Washington DC, killing almost 3,000 people.

This led the United States, under the leadership of George W. Bush, to declare Afghanistan, one of the world's poorest countries, an enemy that had attacked the "free world"—even though not one of the attackers had been an Afghan. The war drums began to sound, and they became virtually impossible to ignore.

On September 11, 2001, I was nine years old and living in Innsbruck, Austria, the city of my birth. Around two years earlier, my family and I had obtained Austrian citizenship. I hadn't yet seen much of the world beyond the Tyrolean Alps, and I knew almost nothing about my Afghan homeland. As I returned home that day, eager to watch my usual cartoons, I was disappointed to find my parents glued to the screen, entranced by a special program being broadcast on all channels. Featuring falling towers in New York and panicked reporters live on air, this program did not stop, and my parents seemed worried. Then, a picture of a bearded man wearing a turban appeared. Though my knowledge of Afghanistan was limited, I knew that *Osama bin Laden* was not an Afghan name. However, he apparently had something to do with the *Taliban*, which ruled over wide swaths of Afghanistan at the time. I didn't know then how much these two terms, bin Laden and Taliban, would haunt me in the coming days and years. Yet on September 12, 2001, I suddenly became "the Afghan" at school, someone with whom not even the Turks, Bosnians, and Serbs wanted to associate.

"Emran, you're from Afghanistan," one of my teachers said to me. "Do you know why they did this?" I didn't take her question personally at the time. Maybe she thought: "He has some sort of Afghanistan connection. Sure, he's just a kid, but maybe he has an answer." Stuttering, I tried to get something out, to set something straight. "But bin Laden isn't an Afghan ... My parents said so ...," I managed. In retrospect, I think this was probably the beginning of a long development that made me what I am today: a perpetual explainer of the war in my homeland. Afghanistan remained the topic of conversation in the break after our lesson. My classmates thought my country needed to be bombed, that we "deserved it." "World War Three," atomic bombings, and all kinds of potential horror scenarios were drawn on the board. "They're going to crush you and the Taliban!" a number of my peers told me, while others asked, "Is Osama bin Laden your uncle?" Today I know that this experience was not unique to me, and that it is still happening. During the Taliban takeover in August 2021, my niece—who was nine years old at the time, as I had been on September 11th—was mobbed by some of her schoolmates who called her "Taliban girl." Since 2001, a wave of anti-Islam sentiment had been growing throughout the Western world, and many children were tormented, harassed, and bullied for being Muslim or simply for being perceived as such. That being said, there were numerous dimensions to this phenomenon, some of which remain unaddressed by scholarship on racism to this day. A student with Turkish roots became a target of our classmates' attacks, yet as soon as someone else was around who was easier to associate with bin Laden and the Taliban, this student quickly switched sides and antagonized the new victim—a Pakistani, an Afghan, or an Iraqi. Often I was this victim, and since I was the only Afghan far and wide, I ultimately bore the brunt of all the hatred and loathing. My classmates had suddenly become war-hungry and racist. But in the end, they were only children, and children usually imitate adults. Today, most of the cluelessness and ignorance I have to deal with comes from historians, columnists, journalists, and politicians.

In contrast to the attitudes I encountered at school, there was a palpably growing sense of fear in my family that the United States would attack Afghanistan, an outcome that seemed increasingly inevitable. Suddenly, people were worried not only about relatives in the line of fire but also about completely unknown compatriots possibly being killed by air strikes. For me, this was a novel, distressing feeling. "*My country* is going to be bombed," I thought to myself again and again. There were days when the stress crushed me. The people around me thirsted for revenge and positively yearned for war, making me increasingly unsettled and nervous. In fact, these attitudes were not unique to my social environment but were common in many Western countries. Hardly anyone questioned an invasion of Afghanistan. Even leading geopolitical institutions such as the United Nations rubber-stamped the war that George W. Bush referred to at the time as a "crusade." An illegal assault on a country, a collective punishment of an entire people who had nothing to do with the attacks in the United States, was simply declared legal. NATO's *casus foederis* came into effect, which was widely viewed even outside of military and political circles as apparently the most normal thing in the world. Rep. Barbara Lee of California was the only member of the US House of Representatives to vote against authorizing the use of military force. "I do not want to see this spiral out of control. [...] If we rush to launch a counterattack, we run too great a risk that women, children, and other non-combatants will be caught in the crossfire," Lee said at the time, warning of "an open-ended war" without an "exit strategy." In response, she was ridiculed, scorned, and labeled a terrorist sympathizer—a term that became widespread in the following years.[1]

October 7, 2001, marked the start of the longest war in American history. Of course, no one knew it would turn out that way at the time. Bombs fell throughout Afghanistan, and armed drones were deployed in the country for the first time. On the ground, US special forces allied with various Afghan warlords, drug barons, and any number of other dubious actors whose biographies belie the notion that Washington and its allies were concerned with democracy and human rights. The Taliban regime was brought down in short order. Even years later, Claus Kleber, the nightly news anchor of the German public television station ZDF, claimed that "the Afghans" had welcomed the American intervention. Attempting to put critics of the NATO deployment in their place, Kleber alleged to have witnessed their reactions himself while reporting in Kabul. In December 2009, two months after more than 150 civilians in Kunduz Province were killed by an air strike ordered by the German colonel Georg Klein, the ZDF correspondent Hans-Ulrich Gack parroted the newspeak of Washington and other war parties by suggesting that the German military was proceeding "too gently" and that "many Afghans" would welcome a tougher approach.[2] Rather than question this kind of rhetoric as a journalist, he spread it with zeal, even quoting the corrupt, NATO-appointed police chief of Kunduz to the effect that the Afghans needed to be "brought into line with the German military and federal government." Journalists such as Kleber and Gack, who knew virtually nothing about Afghanistan and yet constantly flaunted the little they did know, were probably also one of the reasons I eventually took up writing myself and became a war reporter. Western coverage of the war frustrated me—and not only as it pertained to Afghanistan. Often it was characterized by ignorance or racist and Orientalist stereotypes; even to speak of "the Afghans" reveals great ignorance given the heterogeneity of the various groups living within the borders of today's Afghanistan, though many Western journalists think they can draw universally valid conclusions from what they observe in urban centers such as Kabul. Additionally, this coverage was hindered by linguistic and cultural barriers that were rarely broken, either by Kleber or other renowned journalists from Western outlets. As late as 2020, the *New York Times* announced that its freshly appointed Kabul bureau chief intended to learn "a bit of Dari."[3] This reveals not only naïveté, but also ignorance. I know no other case in which such a prominent publication has made a similar announcement before sending a correspondent to Washington, London, or Paris. In part, the failure of Western war coverage to transcend linguistic and cultural barriers has to do with the belief that foreign correspondents must constantly maintain a certain distance to their work environment for the sake of objectivity. That being said, the fact that the results of this coverage are often anything other than objective is usually ignored. In Afghanistan and other theaters of the War on Terror, such mistakes have been constantly repeated in recent years, and they have had devastating consequences. Along these lines, Kleber was of course right to suggest that many Afghans had welcomed the fall of the regime that had repressed their personal freedoms for years. Men shaved their beards, and many women shed their burqas. However, most Afghans live not in cities but the countryside—and the reactions in rural regions were completely different. Here, people were not able to rejoice at the fall of the Taliban regime, as they were the ones being hunted, bombed, and massacred by the Americans and their allies.

An Afghan from Patika or Kandahar had an entirely different experience of the invasion than his compatriot in Kabul. While many in the Afghan capital were celebrating to loud music, others were forced to flee the bombs of US fighter jets. The mere fact that it remains unknown how many Afghans were killed in the air strikes in this first phase of invasion speaks volumes. No one bothered to count them. Nevertheless, it has been established that some of the most brutal war crimes in recent Afghan history took place during those days. Over the following months, courageous journalists documented further atrocities, some of which I caught wind of even as a child. Evenings in our apartment, my parents typically watched the news or documentary reports, especially when they were about Afghanistan. I vaguely remember one documentary where an elderly Afghan wept as he recounted the brutalities to which he was subjected after being imprisoned by the US military. He had been locked in a room and sexually abused by multiple soldiers. It was visibly difficult for him to talk about his experiences. Not only in Afghan culture is it taboo for a man to speak openly about such things. The interview was heartbreaking. My parents sat glued to the couch, suppressing their tears. Even then, it became clear to me that the West's invasion of Afghanistan would not end the barbarity in the country. Rather, the foreign powers would once again become the barbarians themselves—just as had happened with the British and Soviets. At the same time, I felt an urge to report on this war myself one day. Tellingly, voices like that of the nameless elderly man have continued to be ignored since then, almost as if they never existed. Instead, much of Western reporting still focuses on the well-known villains such as the Taliban or—once it had expanded to Afghanistan—the so-called Islamic State of Iraq and Syria (ISIS), which emerged as a direct consequence of the murderous and devastating War on Terror.

Often, attempts are made to "Afghanize" the violence, to claim that we—read, we in the West—have nothing to do with it all. We only want to help, but the barbarians keep butchering each other. This narrative is repeated on a constant loop, the victims of Western violence portrayed as collateral damage whom no one really wanted to kill. Blame is usually pinned on the other side, the latest massacre justified by invoking "human shields" or some other excuse. This too is nothing new. Whoever reads reports by the British colonialists who tried to conquer Afghanistan will realize that they often hardly differ from the contemporary coverage of the country by a number of respected media outlets.

"In the past we would get upset at little arguments and dwell on them for days. Now people are dying every day, and no one cares," a woman from Kabul told me several years ago in an interview. She reveled in nostalgia as she recalled her days as a schoolgirl during the 1970s in the then-peaceful capital. Several years later, her country was invaded by the Soviets. Since their defeat, Afghanistan has been known as the "graveyard of empires." Though there's some truth to this designation, the superpowers have mostly made Afghanistan into a graveyard of Afghans. All the nameless civilians killed over the past two decades are one reason why the United States and its allies stand as losers today. "Who knows what I would have done if foreign powers invaded my country. I probably would have taken up arms too and defended myself," the US military veteran and author Erik Edstrom told me several years ago.[4] During Edstrom's one-year deployment in Afghanistan, he eventually started to understand the people fighting against him. Radicalization, extremism, and militancy aren't unique attributes of the Afghans' nature, though this Orientalist trope has been used to "analyze" various develop-ments for years. What this means concretely was described by the Palestinian-American literary theorist Edward Said more than four decades ago. In his comprehensive work *Orientalism*, Said made clear that Eurocentric views have for centuries determined Western conceptions of the so-called Orient, of which Afghanistan is often considered a part. One might have thought that such views and prejudices would have been eradicated from the world by the twenty-first century. Instead, however, the very theories and narratives that Said and countless others criticized and deconstructed were not only revived but purposely exploited to oppress the populations of Afghanistan and Iraq. An example of this can be seen in the work of the British historian Bernard Lewis, once famous for his debates with Said. Lewis welcomed the War on Terror and explicitly endorsed a US invasion of Iraq on multiple occasions. In an interview with the renowned US journalist Michael Hirsh, Lewis described the September 11 attacks as "the opening salvo of the final battle" between Western and Islamic civilization. For him, brutal wars of aggression against Muslim countries were a necessity.[5]

What Lewis's vision means in practice has now become apparent in Afghanistan: years of constant air strikes and drone attacks, brutal night raids ending in extralegal executions, a corrupt government apparatus, and systematic torture in places such as Guantánamo and Bagram near Kabul massively strengthened the Taliban in the end, ultimately setting the stage for their almost immediate takeover of the government after the US withdrawal in August 2021. The excesses of violence committed by the Western military powers in recent years have returned like a boomerang, a phenomenon that specialists refer to as "blowback." This is apparent not only in Afghanistan but on a global scale. Extremist actors such as the Taliban are a major part of the problem. However, they are primarily a symptom and not the cause. The wars in Afghanistan have influenced generations of Islamists around the world. This is true not only of the brutal American war in the Hindu Kush but the Soviet war as well, which is also discussed in this book.

"We do not want colonialism from the West or the East," young Islamist leaders in Kabul proclaimed as early as the 1960s, a time when they were still fairly marginal. Later, these same reactionary forces rallied hundreds of thousands of Afghans to fight the Soviet occupiers in their homeland. Two million Afghans were killed during the decade of Soviet occupation, while many more were forced to flee through various different countries as refugees. It's mistaken to think that Afghanistan has recovered from that murderous war. In fact, numerous occurrences from the 1970s and 1980s are intimately entangled with the present: a war on terror was already propagated back then, only by Moscow and the Communist dictatorships in Kabul. In this context, it's worth noting how Washington's and Moscow's respective wars are perceived. I can't remember meeting even a single Afghan who did not approve of the uprising against the Red Army and Afghan rebels killing Soviet soldiers. This is true even among representatives of those camps that were allied with Moscow during the Cold War. "The jihad against the Soviets was legitimate," multiple Afghan ex-Communists have told me over the years. Whoever killed Russians is considered a hero who did nothing wrong. Tellingly, the US occupation is already discussed in similar terms. Here as well—and this might be an inconvenient truth for some Western observers—many Afghans draw a clear distinction between the NATO soldiers and the Afghan security forces who were killed. The former are essentially seen as foreign occupiers with no business in Afghanistan. Paradoxically, one even hears this sentiment—off the record, of course—from former officials and representatives of the Kabul government who depended on Western troops during their two decades in power.

Above all, this book aims to clarify Afghan perspectives on matters while deconstructing some of the myths and falsehoods surrounding the wars in Afghanistan that continue to be spread by Western media to this day. It seeks to illustrate why Afghanistan should not be treated as a blank surface onto which people project their own Eurocentrism in order to justify various political agendas. Afghanistan is a wonderful country with an extremely complex history and heterogenous society. In many respects, it evades categorization as left or right, as liberal or traditional. Though such terms are often thrown around, this has more to do with Western discourses and modes of thought—and these have caused tremendous damage in recent decades, in Afghanistan and elsewhere. Their usage reflects the West's dominance in knowledge production. Most authors of well-known English-language books, scholarly articles, and journalistic pieces about Afghanistan are not Afghans. Some of them are renowned thinkers whose expertise I value. Many others, however, have more or less exploited Afghanistan for their own professional advancement. They rarely take off their Eurocentric glasses while they profit from war and human suffering, and they act not infrequently as indirect representatives of the West's military-industrial complex. In practice, this means that their assessments and analyses tend to correspond to those of the actors who benefit from war—that is, with the arms industry, intelligence agencies, the military, and politicians. For this reason, this book explicitly seeks to bring the Afghan perspective to bear on past conflicts in the country, and especially on those that have been unfolding since the 2001 US invasion. As many readers may have been influenced by Western media coverage themselves, presenting this entirely different point of view can be thought of as an act of reclaiming in its own right.

For more than a decade, I have been reporting about and from Afghanistan. During my regular trips, I have made the conscious decision to spend time not only in Kabul but also in places rarely visited by other journalists, including Afghan journalists themselves. The fact that I myself have Afghan heritage has usually played an important, constructive role over the course of my research and reporting. My approach differs quite fundamentally from most of my Western colleagues. I have never stayed in a high-security hotel in Afghanistan or behind thick concrete walls. Normally I have gotten around with the simple taxis used by the majority of the population, not with bulletproof SUVs and armed security personnel. Rarely is it mentioned that foreign journalists in Afghanistan have to follow strict security procedures that ultimately render "normal" reporting nearly impossible in many respects. A good example of this is the "embedded journalism" paradigm, where privileged reporters have accompanied soldiers on operations while always staying within military structures. This has usually resulted in mostly friendly relationships to the troops, zero contact to the local population, and reporting that has been anything other than nuanced. Most news outlets ultimately disseminate coverage that is extremely filtered and incomplete in many respects. Moreover, while the real, dangerous work is mostly done by local journalists for starvation wages, their foreign colleagues are the ones who get to take credit.

The United States and its allies attacked Afghanistan in the name of human rights (and especially women's rights), democracy, freedom of the press, and establishing the rule of law. This book seeks to make clear that Washington, London, Berlin, and so on—read, the West—effectively failed at every one of these goals. Worse still, this failure may have been consciously anticipated from the outset. Not only were the West's own constantly professed values violated in the most brutal ways possible in Afghanistan, the war cry shook the foundations of constitutionality in the states of the Western alliance. In the War on Terror, torture and mass murder were effectively legalized, and hundreds of thousands of people were declared outlaws. Civilians who were hunted and murdered by drones or shadowy special forces units were declared "terrorists"; some even had weapons planted on them to make the claim appear plausible. All these things must be viewed as crimes—and would be considered as such under any existing Western constitution. Yet the West's own progressiveness did not apply to the "barbarians." The West was, in an Orwellian sense, "more equal than others"—and remains so to this day.

While the Afghans were lied to with empty promises of democracy, basic democratic achievements were dismantled in Western countries. Their governments lied to themselves and their citizens. The War on Terror has crystallized the dystopianism of the world we inhabit. Fighting terrorism has become a pretext not only (or even primarily) for hunting down obvious perpetrators, but for systematically monitoring entire populations. The fundamental rights of millions of citizens are being trodden upon, and the various algorithms that have shaped our daily lives for years make it nearly impossible to escape the global surveillance apparatus. This surveillance apparatus has been massively expanded over the last twenty years, and it has made our world less safe, not safer. Similarly—and this is perhaps the most important premise of this book—the Afghanistan War has not eliminated terror but has instead contributed greatly to its spread.

How the Crusade Began

The Godfather of Jihad

IN JULY 2001, Waheed Mozhdah received a visit in his dusty, sparsely furnished office at the Foreign Ministry in Kabul. Several young men wanted to see him and drink tea with him. This in itself was nothing unusual. Mozhdah, a Taliban civil servant in his mid-forties at the time, regularly received visitors from all over the world, including journalists, researchers, Afghanistan enthusiasts, and other interested parties. He assumed a calm and sober demeanor as soon as he began analyzing political events in his country. Mozhdah usually stared into space while giving interviews. Even back then, he dazzled not only with his encyclopedic knowledge but also his strong command of English. For some foreigners, he was reason enough to travel to Kabul—even though the Taliban regime in Kabul was now in its fifth year. This regime was the preliminary result in a long chain of events.

In 1992, the mujahideen rebels toppled Kabul's last Communist regime. Mohammad Najibullah, the deposed regime's leader, had managed to stay in power for three years following the withdrawal of the Soviets. This owed mainly to major financial assistance

1

from Russia and the support of Kabul's military apparatus, which Moscow had spent years building. Yet the effects of perestroika ultimately made themselves felt in Afghanistan as well, and Kabul fell to the rebels. Najibullah led a dictatorial regime. Before becoming Afghanistan's president, he oversaw torture as the director of Kabul's infamous, KGB-built intelligence agency KHAD (Persian: *Khadamat-e Aetla'at-e Dawlati*, English: State Intelligence Agency). Just like his predecessors, Najibullah was ultimately only able to rule thanks to Moscow's blessing. However, in Kabul and the country's other urban centers, there was a certain degree of security. Many citizens, including some who secretly fraternized with the rebels, may even have viewed this status quo as an improvement over the previous years. Najibullah was the fourth and final leader of Kabul's Communist government. But while many Afghans in the capital were content, the country's economic troubles escalated as Russian support waned. Simultaneously, the brutal war raged on in many rural parts of the country. Though Najibullah presented himself to the masses as a patriotic, peace-loving man, he could revert in seconds to the Torturer in Chief who had mutilated his prisoners and kicked them to death.[6] His combination of charisma, pragmatism, and brutality was valued by many of his associates and comrades. Yet when Najibullah's mujahideen enemies captured Kabul in 1992, it also probably gave them reason to doubt his gestures towards peace and calls for a "national reconciliation." In 1996, the mujahideen government was toppled by the Taliban. Still in Kabul at the time, Najibullah was tortured by the extremists and brutally executed.

Once the mujahideen had taken Kabul, Mozhdah returned to the capital. During the 1970s, he had studied economics at the University of Kabul, where he became especially interested in the impact of Abdul Majid Zabuli, the "father of Afghan capitalism." Though there was no war in Afghanistan at the time, many of the subsequent conflicts had already begun to map themselves out. Thanks to several reforms implemented by the king, Mohammad Zahir Shah, the country had developed into a parliamentary monarchy by that point. Elections had been held for the first time in the 1960s, and representatives elected by the people had been debating each other in Afghan parliament. The political landscape consisted of monarchists, republican nationalists, youthful social democratic movements, Communists, Maoists, traditional conservative forces, and Islamists of various stripes. At the same time, while the country was dominated by immense poverty and hunger, the Kabul bourgeoisie were living in a sort of parallel universe. Two particularly important forces in these years were Islamists and Communists. They clashed at the university and elsewhere, and not only with words. Violent confrontations broke out time and again, and like many of his fellow students, Mozhdah observed the goings-on with consternation. In 1973, Mohammad Daoud Khan, the cousin of the king, carried out a bloodless coup while the monarch was on vacation in Italy. The monarchy was abolished, and Daoud proclaimed the first Afghan republic. Yet he also entered into an alliance with the Afghan Communists and became friendlier towards the Soviet Union. The situation deteriorated over the course of the following years. Daoud went after both his Communist allies and Islamist forces while continuing to insist on Afghanistan's sovereignty on the international stage. In one meeting, his behavior provoked the anger of Soviet leader Leonid Brezhnev. When Brezhnev tried to dictate to Daoud how he should guard his northern border with the Soviet Union, the Afghan president abruptly broke off the discussion and left the conference, his pride wounded. He may well have signed his own death warrant by doing so. In April 1978, the Afghan Communists staged a coup, murdering Daoud and his family. The Red Army marched into the country one year later.

Shortly after the Soviets invaded in December 1979, Mozhdah took up arms and joined the resistance along with tens of thousands of other Afghans. During the jihad—that is, the armed Muslim struggle against the Soviet occupation and the Communist regime in Kabul—Mozhdah spent several years in Pakistan and Iran, mainly focusing on his work as a journalist and commentator. He wrote about the war in his homeland, analyzing events as they unfolded. While living in Peshawar, he met a man whom the whole world would come to know years later: Osama bin Laden, or as he was called at the time, Abu Abdallah (Arabic: Father of Abdallah). For Mozhdah and most other Afghans back then, the tall Arab was a nobody to whom they paid little attention. Rather, the situation was the other way around. Arab war tourists wanted to see the men who were making life difficult for the godless Communists despite being sparsely armed. Already in the 1980s, a number of myths and legends had been spun around the mujahideen. To the Politburo in Moscow and its puppet regime in Kabul, they were "terrorists." To most adversaries of the Soviet Union, and above all to the United States and their Western allies, they were "freedom fighters." To Muslims from other countries such as the rich Gulf states, the mujahideen were the embodiment of the ideal Muslim man: pure holy warriors who were prepared to die for their faith. And to many Afghans, they were a mixture of all the above. Supporters and sympathizers of the Kabul regime constantly disparaged them as *ashraar*, or scoundrels, while the masses regarded them as pious freedom fighters and supported them accordingly. The mujahideen were not a homogenous mass but rather came from different social and sectarian backgrounds. There were groups of mujahideen from various tendencies of Islam—that is, of Sunni, Shia, and Sufi Muslims (who are de facto also Sunni Muslims). Many of these men had been simple peasants and workers, although there were also a number of students, engineers, and doctors.

When the mujahideen captured Kabul, many Afghans hoped the war would end. Instead, precisely the opposite happened. The conflict entered into its next phase as the various rebel groups began to fight each other. What followed were some of the darkest days in the history of the Afghan capital. Although many mujahideen had laid down their weapons after the Soviets withdrew, many remaining fighters from various factions now rampaged through Kabul, plundering, raping, and murdering as they went. The streets reeked of death and rotting corpses, while young women threw themselves from the roofs of Soviet-built prefab high-rises to avoid falling into the hands of the armed men greedily prowling after them. "I was a child during the civil war years in the nineties. My mother covered my eyes when we'd walk through the streets. She didn't want me to see all the corpses. But I could smell them and hear the flies feeding and rats gnawing on them," a resident of Kabul told me during an interview. Amidst all this, the splintered mujahideen government was attempting to set up a provisional government. Mozhdah, who had returned to Kabul after his prolonged absence, was appointed to a position in the foreign ministry where he was mainly responsible for the Middle East and North Africa. During his time in Pakistan, he had encountered many Arab volunteers—today we would speak of jihadis who were looking to join the mujahideen. Most of them were working as doctors, teachers, or cooks. Only a fraction were prepared to fight. These men were led by Abdullah Azzam, a radical Palestinian preacher considered *the* mastermind of armed jihad in the twentieth century. Azzam's charisma is seen as unrivaled to this day, and not only in militant Islamist circles. Within a few years, he had been joined by numerous men, many of whom had sought out his Services Bureau for Arab Mujahideen (Arabic: *Maktab Khadamāt al-Mujāhidīn al-'Arab*) in Peshawar after hearing about Soviet atrocities. One of these men—albeit later in the war—was Osama bin Laden, who became Azzam's mentee. As Mozhdah recalls, "Abdullah Azzam was a rhetorical genius. Many men left his speeches feeling enlightened in a certain sense. They saw many things more clearly and wanted to follow this man."

Azzam's biography has been written numerous times over the years, and it can help shed light onto the different jihadi currents present in many parts of the world to this day. During the Six-Day War in 1967, Azzam fled from the West Bank to Jordan. He would remain a refugee the rest of his life, never again returning to his Palestinian homeland. Already at the time, Azzam was strongly influenced by the Egypt-based Muslim Brotherhood, an Islamist group with revolutionary ideals. He admired their ideology and increasingly came to despise that of the secular Arab nationalists, whom he held partially responsible for the plight of Palestine. During the founding of Israel, the eight-year-old Azzam directly witnessed the deployment of many Arab militias. These were mostly composed not of Islamists but secular Arabs, including many non-Muslims, not to mention soldiers who drank alcohol and used drugs. "True Islam did not enter the battles of 1948," Azzam later commented.[7]

At the start of his exile, Azzam held several teaching posts in Arab countries and developed into an Islamist preacher seeking to free the Muslim world from its occupiers. In addition to the Israelis, who had made him homeless, he also gave speeches attacking the Americans, British, and Soviets—not to mention the Arab nationalist leaders, whom he regarded as blasphemers for their secular worldview and affinity towards the Soviet Union. Azzam toured through numerous countries to drum up support for his "great war" against the West (which for him included the Soviet Union). It was during these travels that he met his later student bin Laden for the first time, though this happened not in Pakistan near the Afghan border, as one might expect, but probably instead—as unimaginable as it may sound today—in an Islamic educational center in Indianapolis, Indiana, in 1978.[8] Back then, Islamist preachers could move considerably more freely and recruit with greater ease. American security agencies were more focused on Communism than potential Islamist enemies. Both sides knew that they could use each other for their own ends. This is especially obvious in the case of the Afghan warlord and mujahideen leader Gulbuddin Hekmatyar and his party, Hizb-e Islami, which attracted hundreds of thousands of Afghan members.

Hekmatyar was one of the Kabul regime's archenemies. As early as his student years, he had made a name for himself as a Communist hunter, gaining numerous followers. In at least one instance during the Daoud era, the young Hekmatyar was even accused of murder. Following a confrontation between left-wing and Islamist students, a young Maoist by the name of Saydal Sokhandan was found dead. Several sources alleged that the perpetrator was actually an admirer of Hekmatyar's named Mohammad Karim, yet the latter was never prosecuted, and Hekmatyar and other young Islamist leaders were arrested by the Daoud regime. This only contributed to the growing heroization of Hekmatyar and his followers. From his jail cell, Hekmatyar received a steady stream of visits and piles of gifts.[9] His party was one of the main recipients of Western money during the war against the Soviet Union, thanks in part to the Pakistani intelligence agency, ISI (Inter-Services Intelligence). Though he remained a radical who despised the West, he was well aware of the role he had to play. Similar to Azzam, albeit somewhat more famous and popular in various Muslim circles, Hekmatyar toured through numerous countries. In West Germany, he had meetings with the Bavarian Minister-President Franz Josef Strauss and former chancellor Willy Brandt. He made speeches to Muslims in Munich and other cities about the atrocities of the Red Army. Yet he also warned his audiences about the "other colonialists," read, the Western states, emphasizing that they were pursuing not a noble mission in Afghanistan but simply their own interests.[10] Hekmatyar made a point of canceling a meeting with President Ronald Reagan. When the US and its allies invaded Afghanistan almost two decades later, he declared war on them. From then on, Gulbuddin Hekmatyar was considered a "terrorist" by Washington and its allies.

Azzam's Services Bureau maintained close contact with Hekmatyar and other mujahideen leaders. Eventually it became the hub in Peshawar for "Afghan Arabs," as the foreign mujahideen fighters were called. Numbering in the thousands, these men played an insignificant role on the battlefield against the Soviets. The war was fought mainly by the Afghans themselves, and no small amount of Azzam's fighters were alienated by their customs and traditions. The majority of Afghans are Sunni Muslims of the Hanafi school of Islamic Law. In contrast, the adherents of the three other schools of Sunni Islamic law—the Maliki, the Hanbali, and the Shafi'i—are mostly from North Africa and the Arabian Peninsula. Some of the religious practices that were widespread among Afghan Muslims were viewed critically by the Arabs. For example, they looked down on shrine visitation, a common practice in the region for centuries.

Azzam encouraged understanding by educating his fighters about the realities on the ground and instructing them to respect local customs. The last thing he wanted was a sectarian conflict between Muslims. Thanks to his successes in the militant Islamist scene, Abdullah Azzam is today regarded as a kind of godfather of global jihad. Many of the jihadi terror groups that plague various countries today, including Osama bin Laden's Al Qaeda, can be traced back to him in one way or another. From another perspective, however, even Azzam's Services Bureau was heterogenous, and more radical forces—today we would speak of Salafi jihadis—soon tried to pursue their own agenda. A particularly problematic development can be seen in the figure of Ayman al-Zawahiri, an Egyptian doctor who would become famous as Al Qaeda's second in command. Before departing for Pakistan, experiences in Egypt had turned al-Zawahiri into a committed extremist who adhered to the ideology of *takfir*, excommunicating individuals and entire groups from Islam, declaring them non-Muslims, and green-lighting their executions. Even many of the Afghan mujahideen who had fought the Soviets were viewed by al-Zawahiri and his followers as lost people who had in some cases long since fallen away from the faith. The *takfiris* around al-Zawahiri, who had recruited the wealthy Osama bin Laden for financial reasons, eventually began to turn on the teachings of Abdullah Azzam. There is no doubt that Azzam was himself a radical preacher, and it is not for nothing that his reputation as the leading figure of global armed jihad has lasted. He was the mastermind of movements that spread fear and terror to this day. Yet at the same time, he was also a symptom of a much larger problem. Azzam viewed the Soviet Union, the United States, Israel (the country that had made him a refugee), and the secular nationalist dictatorships of the Arab world as enemies of Muslims who had to be fought. On multiple occasions, he argued at length that the Soviet invasion of Afghanistan was a textbook example of something that demanded "defensive jihad," a duty of every Muslim similar to daily prayer or fasting during the month of Ramadan. Azzam was hardly alone in his reasoning. The attacks and massacres by the Red Army and their Afghan Communist allies in Kabul were for him a major assault on the Muslim faith in Afghanistan.

Azzam and other preachers followed events closely, using war crimes as evidence for their arguments and growing increasingly popular. "When I heard about all the Soviet atrocities, I had to cry. I couldn't stay passive," Mohamedou Ould Slahi, the author of *Guantánamo Diary*, told me years later.[11] The native Mauritanian was one of many Muslims who had traveled to Afghanistan to fight on the front in the late 1980s. In 2002, Slahi was abducted for his alleged links to Al Qaeda extremists and taken to the newly erected Guantánamo Bay detention camp, where he was detained without charge and tortured for fourteen years.

Azzam sought to reunite Muslims in the face of a common enemy, yet he was stymied by the sectarian activities of his co-religionists. A further example of his anti-sectarian sensibility can be seen in his behavior towards the two largest Afghan mujahideen parties: Hizb-e Islami, which was led by Gulbuddin Hekmatyar, and Jamiat-e Islami, led by Burhanuddin Rabbani and Ahmad Shah Massoud. All of these men earned themselves reputations as brutal warlords and destroyers of Kabul while fighting each other in the civil war years following the Soviet withdrawal. The conflict between their parties, however, went back to the jihad against the Soviets. Azzam had made multiple attempts to diffuse the conflict in order to prevent a future civil war in Afghanistan. Yet these efforts were in vain, and in November 1989, Abdullah Azzam was killed by a car bomb in Peshawar. The day before the murder, Mozhdah had noticed a cleaning crew in the neighborhood of Peshawar that was home to Azzam's office and a mosque attended by Arabs. The crew was probably a hit squad in disguise that had installed a bomb in an underground water pipe. The pipe detonated the next day as Azzam drove past it on his way to Friday prayers, killing him and two of his sons, Mohammad and Ibrahim. The masterminds behind the attack remain unknown, though many observers have suggested different culprits, including the CIA, Mossad, Pakistan's ISI, Afghanistan's KHAD, and even the extremist forces around Ayman al-Zawahiri and Osama bin Laden. The latter benefitted de facto from the murder, which cleared the way for them to establish the group that has since been known as Al Qaeda. Numerous confidants of Azzam, including his son Hutaifa and his son-in-law, the journalist and book author Abdullah Anas, have claimed time and again that had Azzam lived, there would have been no Al Qaeda or September 11. In his 2019 book, *To the Mountains*, Anas writes at length about his time with Azzam in Pakistan and Afghanistan.[12] His narrative draws a clear division between the concept of jihad at the time and the perversion of this concept by groups such as Al Qaeda in subsequent years.[13]

At some point during Mozhdah's meeting with the young men in the summer of 2001, it occurred to him that his visitors were not Afghans. They spoke with him in fluent Pashto, but one of the men answered a phone call in Arabic. Mozhdah asked him where he was from. "I'm actually an Algerian," he answered. Years later, Mozhdah would claim that he knew at that moment that the man was a member of bin Laden's Al Qaeda. Over the course of the conversation, he and Mozhdah discussed the role of the US after the fall of the Iron Curtain and American imperialism in the Muslim world. Eventually, the Algerian smiled and left Mozhdah's office with ominous parting words: "We've planned something big—and soon the whole world will be talking about our struggle." Mozhdah had no idea what he meant, but the whole affair made him uneasy. He went to his boss at the time, the Taliban regime's foreign minister, Ahmad Muttawakil. Most mujahideen leaders had gone into exile when the Taliban captured Kabul in 1996, but their chaotic governing apparatus remained partially intact, and several officials such as Mozhdah had stayed in the capital. These few remaining experts, some of whom were ex-mujahideen or former Communists, were essential for the Taliban. After all, many Taliban warriors had grown up in Pakistani refugee camps or isolated Afghan villages and knew little about the wider world, let alone how to run a country. Muttawakil took the Algerian's statement with a grain of salt. The Arabs around bin Laden "are all crazy anyway," he told Mozhdah.[14] Bin Laden had already been living in Afghanistan for five years at the time. He had been helped back into the country by high-ranking mujahideen leaders, some of whom were from the circles around the

warlords Burhanuddin Rabbani and Abdul Rab Rasoul Sayyaf—
two of the US's closest allies in the Hindu Kush from the end of
2001 onward.[15] The Taliban had continued to host him for reasons
of intra-Muslim fraternity and Afghan hospitality, though he was
increasingly becoming a thorn in their side. Though the Taliban may
have been reactionary extremists themselves, they were pursuing
a national agenda and were well aware of Afghanistan's economic
dependence on foreign powers, including the US. Bin Laden, on the
other hand, declared war on the Americans from Afghan soil. During
the 1990s, Al Qaeda attacks increased, and the group became ever
more globalized. However, the climax of the terror was yet to come.
On September 11, 2001, around two months after the meeting in
Mozhdah's office, nineteen terrorists hijacked several passenger
flights and piloted them into the World Trade Center in New York
and the Pentagon in Washington, DC, killing over 3,000 people.
News of the attack spread like wildfire. When it reached Mozhdah,
he knew immediately what his young Algerian visitor had been
alluding to mere weeks before. He realized that Afghanistan was
about to change forever.

The Man with the Karakul

In the Pakistani city of Quetta near the Afghan border, one man
was following the events in the United States with particular
interest, already anticipating how they might redound to his personal benefit. Hamid Karzai, a middle-aged Pashtun leader, was
basically a nobody back then. Nevertheless, he knew his time
had come. "The Americans will attack the Taliban. We have to
seize the moment," he tried to explain to his relatives and tribe
members. Bearing a striking resemblance to the Indian-British
actor Ben Kingsley, by whom he would later be played, the gaunt,
lanky Karzai was a member of the Popalzai, a Pashtun tribe from
southern Afghanistan. A sub-tribe of the Durrani, the Popalzai are
viewed as the founders of modern Afghanistan. In the eighteenth
century, the Pashtun Ahmad Shah Durrani was named emir of an

empire that encompassed large swaths of present-day Afghanistan, stretching from the steppes of Central Asia to the Delhi Sultanate of northern India. Earlier that same century, another Pashtun by the name of Shah Mahmoud Hotak had led a successful movement for independence from the Persian Empire, a feat that made even the Ottomans nervous. Several decades later, the Durrani Empire had become the second largest Muslim empire in the world.[16] Though ethnically and religiously diverse, its political life had long been dominated by the Durrani Pashtuns. Their leadership would stretch into modern Afghanistan.

The Karzai family are not direct descendants of nobility, but they view themselves as part of this tradition. They have long involved themselves in Afghan politics. Karzai's father, Abdul Ahad, served as deputy speaker of parliament during the era of Afghanistan's last king, Mohammad Zahir Shah. Later, during the Soviet occupation, the elder Karzai supported the mujahideen and spent three years in Communist captivity. The Karzais have been extremely critical of the Pakistani state, which has offered millions of their compatriots exile. The reason for this is historical in nature. Nearly a third of Pakistanis once belonged to the Durrani Empire, which resisted multiple British colonization attempts. However, at the end of the nineteenth century, the British managed to install in Kabul the sympathetic emir Abdur Rahman Khan, helping him to depose his cousin. In 1893, Abdur Rahman signed the Treaty of Durand, named after the British diplomat Sir Mortimer Durand. As a consequence, the territory of Afghanistan was geographically severed from that of the British Empire.

A Machiavellian ruler, Abdur Rahman developed into a brutal tyrant. He quashed all dissent, waged numerous civil wars, deported and executed enemies en masse well before Stalin and other despots, and carried out a genocide against the Hazaras, a predominantly Shia minority group. The point of all this was to make a modern, Western-style Afghan nation-state out of whole cloth—and approving the Durand Line was part of this effort.[17] The new border cut right through the Pashtun tribal areas, which include the provinces of Khyber Pakhtunkhwa, Balochistan with its access to the sea, and the Federally Administered Tribal Areas (FATA, also widely known simply as the Pashtun tribal areas). Half a century later, over the course of India's struggle for independence, parts of these areas were incorporated into the new Pakistani nation-state. This inflicted a trauma from which Afghan Pashtun nationalists such as the Karzais have yet to recover.

Pakistani support for the Afghan resistance was thus a fraught matter for Abdul Ahad Karzai. One of the main beneficiaries of the war against the Soviets, Pakistan's so-called establishment—consisting of politicians, the military, and the infamous ISI—provided the mujahideen and especially Hekmatyar's Hizb-e Islami with massive amounts of weapons and all manner of logistical and financial aid to fight the Red Army and Kabul's Communist regime, allies of Pakistan's archenemy India. The Islamists around Hekmatyar had already received support from Islamabad in the mid-1970s for a possible coup against Daoud Khan, Afghanistan's authoritarian nationalist president. In line with a specific tradition of Kabul leaders, Daoud had been defying Pakistan through intense politicking around the so-called Pashtunistan question—that is, the issue of the tribal areas on the far side of the Durand Line. For Daoud, the point of this was to show the world that the Afghans would not accept a colonialist border. To this day, however, critics see in his and other likeminded nationalists' exclusive focus on the Durand Line and the Pashtun territories a specific ethnocentrism at work, as all borders of modern Afghanistan are de facto colonial borders that have divided peoples.

Either way, Pakistan did not take kindly to Daoud's border politics. In response, it began instrumentalizing Islamists within Afghanistan, who at the time were just starting to organize at and become a thorn in the side of the regent in Kabul. Later in the context of the Cold War, Pakistan would back these same Islamists and men such as Hekmatyar to the hilt. Meanwhile, traditional nationalist leaders such as Abdul Ahad Karzai would fade into the background and became increasingly irrelevant. By that time, the Karzai family was already geographically splintered. Three of Abdul Ahad's sons, Ahmad Wali, Qayoum, and Mahmoud, were living in the United States, dabbling as entrepreneurs in the restaurant business. His son Hamid, however, was mostly by his side.

Speaking with a British accent acquired while studying political science in India, the younger Karzai stood in marked contrast to men such as Hekmatyar and other warlords even back then. He was not a warrior, but a diplomat and politician—the kind of person who evokes the Afghan word *chalbaazi*, which more or less means "to get one over on someone." And Karzai indeed proved to be a sly fox. He knew his people and understood how to use certain realities to his advantage. Yet these defining traits of his would only become apparent in later years. Karzai had spent a long time working for the mujahideen in Pakistan, and when the rebels captured Kabul in 1992, he was appointed deputy foreign minister. He played a rather unimportant role, however, and resigned from his post early. On countless occasions, it became obvious how much Karzai differed from the warlords now holding sway in Kabul. At one point, a dispute arose between him and Burhanuddin Rabbani, the president of the fractured mujahideen government. Karzai was accused of secretly establishing contact with the enemy Hekmatyar, then officially prime minister. While Rabbani and Hekmatyar were firing missiles at each other, Karzai was arrested and brutally interrogated by one of Rabbani's commanders, Mohammad Fahim. Ironically, Fahim would become Karzai's vice president several years later.[18]

After his dispute with Rabbani, Karzai fled to Pakistan yet again. When the Taliban later captured the Afghan capital, he initially welcomed them as a legitimate government, hoping they would bring order to the chaos. Karzai maintained contact with some Taliban officials, and several attempts at rapprochement followed.[19] Yet the Pashtun patriotism of the Karzai family flared up time and again, and Karzai himself grew especially worried about the Pakistani establishment's connections to the budding extremist movement in his homeland. In Quetta in the late 1990s, Karzai found himself back in his old role as a kind of combination bridge builder, diplomat, and willing agent of various interests. To journalists, NGO employees, and Western diplomats, he proved himself a suitable liaison and Afghanistan explainer. He could hold court with them in fluent English while sitting on the floor and interpreting in Persian or Pashto for his fellow tribe members and countrymen. A cosmopolitan through and through, Karzai maintained contact with his family and the broader Afghan diaspora in the US, the Afghan king Mohammad Zahir Shah and his circle in Italian exile, Western embassies in Islamabad, and Pashtun nationalists within Pakistan.

However, most of these actors did not view Hamid Karzai as an important person in Afghanistan. In the words of German UN diplomat Norbert Holl, he was considered a man with "limited potential."[20] Meanwhile, the Karzai family's hereditary distrust of the Pakistani state apparatus persisted. It was further affirmed in July 1999 when unknown gunmen killed Karzai's father, Abdul Ahad, an act that the Karzais blamed on the Taliban and thus indirectly on their Pakistani sponsors. After the murder, Hamid assumed his father's role as tribal chief of the Popalzai. This put him in a position to make the most of his traits after the September 11 attacks. Arming himself with rhetoric instead of weapons, Karzai began to prepare his clan for an impending change of government in Kabul. His goal was to return to his Afghan homeland, then still controlled by the Taliban, where he would rally more supporters. To this end, he focused primarily on the southern provinces of Urzgan, his traditional tribal area, and on the bordering city of Kandahar in his home province, once the capital of the Durrani Empire and now the unofficial center of the Taliban emirate.

While Karzai infiltrated Afghanistan on motorcycle via the Durand Line, other actors were also beginning to move. The White House's war preparations had shifted into high gear, and various possible scenarios were emerging on the horizon. Plans were crystallizing to deploy US special forces units to ally with various US-friendly assets on the ground. Thanks to Karzai's diplomatic legwork, he had made it onto a list of warlords, smugglers, and drug kingpins who were eager for American intervention and the fall of the Taliban regime.

In one National Security Council briefing, Secretary of Defense Donald Rumsfeld floated the "gentle-looking" Karzai's name as a possible Washington ally in southern Afghanistan. "We can get a CIA team in," Director of Central Intelligence George Tenet responded. The war was now in full swing—and so was Karzai's ascent.[21]

While Karzai was making his own plans, alliances were continuing to form. A de facto scramble for power was unfolding. In particular, the warlords from the civil war years were plotting their return, hoping for the biggest piece of the pie. Compared to them, Karzai was indeed a saint. All of the other men whom Washington was eyeing were virtually without exception violent warlords every bit as brutal as the reactionary extremists of the Taliban. In fact, the warlords' reign of terror in the 1990s is what brought the Taliban to power in the first place. This dynamic is captured in miniature in an occurrence now seen as virtually identical with the founding of the Taliban. Back in early 1994, news spread through Kandahar that a local warlord had kidnapped two girls, whom he was harassing, torturing, and raping behind the walls of his fortress. It was said that he'd shaven their heads and was holding them as sex slaves. The inhabitants of the region were powerless to act and completely at the mercy of this man and his militias. When the mullah of a small village mosque learned of the incident, he gathered his students. Lightly armed, they stormed the warlord's fortress, killing him and his troops. The girls were freed, and the mullah and his students were hailed by many Afghans as saviors—at least at first. For the man from the mosque was no one less than Mullah Mohammad Omar, the founder and subsequent leader of the Taliban. In essence, this and subsequent occurrences illustrate that the Taliban were the symptom of a much deeper problem: namely, that the Afghan state was already a warlord empire, having emerged as such from the rubble of Communist dictatorship. The "nation-building" mission of the West exacerbated precisely this problem. Though the West invaded in the name of democracy, freedom, and human rights, it allied itself from day one of the War on Terror with the very warlords and militiamen who had themselves long terrorized the

Afghan people. Fighting in a united front alongside these men, it consciously ignored some of the most brutal war crimes in modern Afghan history while participating in others. This issue still has not been processed. Instead, the opposite has happened. Some of the most notorious Afghan warlords have been glorified as heroes thanks in part to a massive propaganda apparatus by the name of Hollywood. A recent example is the film *12 Strong* from 2018. In the film, US soldiers team up with the infamous warlord Abdul Rashid Dostum to heroically chase off Taliban fighters in what was probably the last cavalry campaign in modern military history. The fact that Dostum is a brutal war criminal who should rightfully be sitting in the dock at The Hague goes unmentioned. From the very first days of deployment, the stocky Dostum counted among the closest allies of the West, even though his fighters had committed numerous war crimes back in the 1980s and early 1990s. Once an army commander of Kabul's Communist regime, he would later fight for virtually all sides in the civil war years before summarily betraying them. He is responsible for a whole host of atrocities, including some in the immediate aftermath of September 11.

In December 2001, Dostum's militias perpetrated the massacre of Dasht-e Laili, a desert in northern Afghanistan. Over the course of the ordeal, thousands of Taliban fighters—in addition to numerous unknown men who simply happened to be in the wrong place at the wrong time—were locked in metal shipping containers and executed. For days, Dostum's men let the containers sit in the desert while they shot holes in their walls. The prisoners experienced the utmost agony while dying of thirst in the heat. When the containers were finally opened, a bestial stench escaped—a mixture of blood, decay, urine, and feces, as eyewitnesses later described it. Approximately 220 men had been crammed into each container, and only a few from each survived the torture. Most of these survivors were then executed. The corpses were deposited in mass graves. As a survivor of the atrocity by the name of Asif Iqbal later recalled, "We lived because someone made holes with a machine gun, though they were shooting low and still more died from the bullets. The last thing I remember is that it got really hot, and everyone started screaming and banging. It was like someone had lit a fire beneath the containers. You could feel the moisture running off your body, and people were ripping off their clothes." Iqbal was completely drained when he awoke, having not had anything to drink for two days. With a piece of fabric, he wiped fluid from the walls of the container and began sucking on it. Eventually, he realized he was drinking the blood of the dead. "We were like zombies. We stank; we were covered in blood and the smell of death."[22]

Dostum personally participated in this unfathomable crime, which US soldiers allowed him to commit. They practically even watched. The Pakistani journalist Ahmed Rashid, known for his numerous bestsellers about the region, has described the massacre of Dasht-e Laili as one of the most brutal war crimes of the entire Afghanistan War. Observers have reported between 4,500 and 7,000 victims.[23] This makes Hollywood's erasure of the incident all the more macabre. *12 Strong* depicts Dostum as a thoughtful freedom fighter and his heroic American allies as exclusively focused on one task: hunting down the evil terrorists and rescuing the "good" Afghans. Its leading role was played by Australian actor Chris Hemsworth, mainly known for starring as the Marvel superhero Thor. The film is sheer hypocrisy and a willful distortion of actual events.

While Dostum was serving as Washington's man in northern Afghanistan, similar scenarios were unfolding across the country. Small teams of US special forces and other NATO troops such as the German Bundeswehr were linking up with men like Dostum to pursue their objectives on the ground by indiscriminately attacking, arresting, torturing, and massacring civilians, most of whom they labeled "terror suspects." Crimes of this sort occurred in Kabul as well, even while many Western outlets were propagating a "positive" image by focusing on people celebrating the fall of the Taliban regime. "From thousands and thousands of miles away, another superpower is dropping bombs on our heads," one victim of the American air attacks in the Afghan capital put it.[24] Besides Dostum, other important allies of the West included the brawny politician and drug kingpin Gul Agha Sherzai, an adversary of Karzai in the Kandahar region; the former mujahideen commanders Ismail Khan, Karim Khalili, Noor Mohammad Atta, and Mohammad Fahim; and the warlord Burhanuddin Rabbani, who had fled to Iran when the Taliban captured Kabul.

Several other well-known warlords were absent from the coalition. Most notable among them was Ahmad Shah Massoud, Rabbani's right-hand man and a former leader of the United Islamic National Front for the Salvation of Afghanistan, an anti-Taliban military front established in the 1990s more widely known as the Northern Alliance. Two days before the September 11 attacks, Massoud was murdered by Al Qaeda assassins disguised as journalists. He had been one of Afghanistan's most famous mujahideen leaders. Western and especially French journalists had marveled at this man with a neatly trimmed goatee and traditional Pakol cap, comparing him to Ho Chi Minh and Che Guevara. This apparently pleased Massoud, who had a penchant for striking Che's heroic pose in photographs and imitating his clothing style. During one trip to Europe, Massoud became one of the few people to warn the West before the September 11 attacks about the danger posed by Al Qaeda and similar groups. In Afghanistan, however, he was and remains a controversial figure, even long after his murder. The government declared him an official state hero at the end of 2001, yet many Afghans still associate him with the brutality of the civil war years, not to mention his dubious ties to foreign actors: instead of fighting the Soviet troops, Massoud struck a kind of peace deal with them, as he did with Pakistan and later also India and Iran. Massoud was considered Hekmatyar's main adversary. In their fight over the capital, these two men destroyed Kabul and traumatized hundreds of thousands of Afghans. During an operation against the Shia mujahideen faction Hizb-e Wahdat in February 1993, the militias of Massoud and Abdul Rab Rasoul Sayyaf committed a massacre in Kabul's Afshar neighborhood, murdering numerous members of the mostly Shia Hazara minority group. It has been reported that more than 5,000 houses were stormed by the militias. Their victims included numerous women and children, many of whose corpses showed signs of mutilation. According to Human Rights Watch, it is impossible to determine the exact number of victims of the Afshar massacre, though there were at least several hundred.[25] Several observers have spoken of an attack on civilians of genocidal proportions. Further massacres of Hazaras were committed by the Taliban after they had come to power.[26] In August 1999, Taliban forces captured Mazar-e Sharif in the north of the country and slaughtered several hundred people including women and children. Other cities in the region which were overran by the militants faced similar fates. Occurrences of this sort have burned themselves into the collective memory of Afghan ethnic groups and have yet to be processed to this day.

Though Massoud posed a problem for several different actors, there is no question that his assassination was linked to the attacks that took place two days later on September 11. Most importantly, he stood in the way of Al Qaeda and Osama bin Laden's grand plan to destroy the American empire by drawing it into a new conflict that would consume resources for years. On May 2, 2011, Osama bin Laden was killed by a team of US Navy SEALs. The operation took place not in Afghanistan but in a house in the Pakistani garrison town of Abbottabad, of all places. Pakistan, which had supported the Americans' War on Terror from the beginning, now found itself in hot water. Many observers still refuse to believe that the ISI knew nothing about bin Laden's whereabouts. After all, the intelligence agency had played a perfidious game since the start of the war, receiving billions in US military aid while also harboring prominent Taliban leaders whom it handed over to be arrested and tortured only when advantageous. Just as it had done in the 1980s, the Pakistani state was advancing its interest in the region by instrumentalizing militant Islamists in Afghanistan. Those who did not comply with Islamabad were punished with bloody military operations or CIA drone attacks, or given up to the Americans.

After the operation to take out bin Laden, a search of his hideout turned up numerous Al Qaeda documents that confirmed the group's "ultimate plan." Having taken shape as early as the 1990s when bin Laden declared war on the United States, it entailed a "strategy of a thousand cuts" that would eventually cause Washington to fall.[27] To this end, bin Laden and his henchmen accepted the suffering of the Afghan population under a potential US occupation as a price that had to be paid. Here it bears mention that Al Qaeda did not play a significant role on the battlefield in Afghanistan. While the Americans were occupying themselves with the Taliban and other Afghan groups, Al Qaeda was successfully expanding in Africa and the Middle East. Twenty years after the start of the War on Terror, it can be said that Al Qaeda's strategy has worked in some respects. The US empire has departed Afghanistan a loser, and the White House is now occupied by Joe Biden—the very man whom bin Laden most wanted to see as president, viewing him as "totally unprepared" for the job. Believing his plan would come to quicker fruition under a Biden administration, bin Laden even considered attempting to assassinate Barack Obama during his visit to Afghanistan.[28] Yet had he lived to see it, bin Laden would have been even more pleased by the rise of Biden's predecessor, Donald Trump.

In contrast to bin Laden, Massoud pursued a decidedly nationalist agenda, rejecting any and all Pakistani influence. Some even claim that he would have actively opposed an American invasion. He would have had the authority and local support to do so at any rate. However, neither Washington nor the many other warlords who benefitted from the US invasion would have cared. Several sources have alleged that the assassins who killed Massoud were connected to Abdul Rab Rasul Sayyaf, the very man who helped bring bin Laden to Afghanistan in the 1990s.[29] Around the same time as Massoud's murder, a man by the name of Abdul Haqq met a similar fate. A well-known former mujahideen commander who maintained close ties to American and British intelligence agencies, Haqq was killed by the Taliban around two weeks prior to the start of the US invasion. He had enjoyed strong support in eastern Afghanistan and was in favor of an intervention against the Taliban. However, it was subsequently revealed that he had already been planning his own coup against the Taliban before the invasion and may not have tolerated a prolonged presence of US troops. His murder was blamed on a Taliban leader named Mawlana Abdul Kabir, who probably acted alone. According to several sources, Haqq maintained close contact with several Taliban leaders. There was a possibility that he might have been able to win them over to his side.[30]

While considering these potentially more "positive" scenarios, it should not be forgotten that both Massoud and Haqq were warlords whose militias have been blamed for numerous human rights violations. Any peace-loving idealist would have preferred seeing them vanish from Afghan politics entirely. Of course, we live in a world of Realpolitik, and both of these men were fixtures of the Afghan political landscape at the time, as was the Taliban. That being said, if creating peace and democracy in Afghanistan had in fact been the goal, the strong influence of the warlords would have needed to be curbed after 2001. Instead, the US strengthened their hand by declaring war on the Taliban, throwing itself into a conflict that would rage for the next two decades. This strategic decision came about during negotiations over the interim regime at the first International Conference on Afghanistan. Held on the Petersberg mountain near Bonn, Germany, on November 27, 2001, its attendees included UN Special Envoy for Afghanistan Lakhdar Brahimi, representatives of the aforementioned warlords and of several other political factions, and Zalmay Khalilzad, an Afghan-American who had had a hand in shaping Washington's policy in the Hindu Kush for years. The Taliban were not present. Their interests were no longer seen as relevant. In their absence, the main winners to emerge from conference were the Northern Alliance and the so-called Rome Group around the former king Zahir Shah, which included Karzai. Burhanuddin Rabbani, the leader of the Northern Alliance member party Jamiat-e Islami, began making arrangements for his return.

The president of Afghanistan during the civil war years, Burhanuddin had continued to view himself during exile as the official head of state, believing that the Taliban's invasion of Kabul had illegally cut short his time in office. Yet the idea of a Rabbani reinstatement was fraught with controversy. Countless Afghans were instead advocating for a return of the king. The situation was further complicated by the country's ethnic composition, an ever growing source of conflict since the 1990s. To this day, the discourse surrounding this issue is dominated by dubious narratives left over from the British colonial era (such as the unfounded view that Afghanistan can only be ruled by a Pashtun), and in 2001, these narratives were exploited by the new occupiers. As a matter of fact, Afghanistan's population is extremely ethnically, culturally, and religiously diverse. Though the dominant group has long been the Pashtuns, the founders of the modern Afghan nation-state, it is unclear whether they actually constitute a majority of the population, as no comprehensive census has ever been conducted. For this same reason, the precise geographic distribution of other ethnic groups such as the Tajiks, the Uzbeks, and the Hazaras is also uncertain. Furthermore, when one takes into account the centuries of intermingling between the various ethnic groups, any attempt to draw hard distinctions becomes increasingly problematic. Yet these realities did not stop old colonial narratives from being resurrected on the Petersberg in 2001. Several years later, similar narratives would famously be used to carve up Iraq chiefly along sectarian lines. This might be seen as a result of what happened in Afghanistan, where Zalmay Khalilzad, himself a Pashtun, pushed for the population to be divided along ethnic lines. To this day, Khalilzad has hardly expressed any regret for his actions. On the contrary, in his 2016 book, *The Envoy*, he repeats exactly the same problematic narratives he used to justify his thinking at the time.[31]

At one point during the Bonn conference, another guest made a surprise appearance. Equipped with a satellite telephone from the CIA, Hamid Karzai was patched in live from the Afghan province of Uruzgan as American bombs fell apace and the Northern Alliance captured Kabul.[32] Virtually none of the attendees took Karzai seriously at the time. Not even his own Rome Group had imagined that he of all people, a man who had never used a weapon in his life, would prevail against all the brutal and battle-hardened men simply on the strength of his diplomatic skills. Yet Karzai checked the right boxes for the architects of the "new Afghanistan." He was a Pashtun who got along well with all sides. He enjoyed a certain degree of support from his tribe, but unlike the warlords, he did not possess his own private army. Karzai was easier to control than these men, and he would prove to be an obedient ally of the West during his first years in office in Kabul. In the end, the Karzai option managed to win over not only the domestic Afghan players at the conference but also those from neighboring states such as Pakistan and Iran, which had treated Afghanistan as little more than a chessboard for years. Surprisingly, the members of Karzai's own Rome Group voted against him. They instead opted for their leader, Abdul Sattar Sirat, a minister under the king decades prior. Sirat was not a Pashtun like Karzai but an ethnic Uzbek. After Karzai was appointed president of the interim government, Sirat fell out with him and blamed him for fueling the growth of Afghan politics along ethnic lines. Yet Karzai paid these accusations no heed. To show off Afghanistan's ethnic diversity, he donned a karakul, a type of hat worn mostly by the country's political elite, and an Uzbek cloak common in the north, which would become his trademark in the coming years. In his speeches, he usually spoke Dari and Pashto so as not to offend anyone. Depending on the narrative one accepts, Karzai had become either the president of the "new" and "democratic" Afghanistan, or alternatively, the "mayor of Kabul," a powerless and corrupt figure surrounded by drug kingpins and warlords vying for influence.

Beyond Kabul: On Bush's Illegal "Crusade" and the "Clash of Cultures"

"This crusade, this war on terrorism is going to take a while." George W. Bush uttered these words before reporters on September 16, 2001, after he had returned from Camp David to the White House. Bush also made several references to the "evildoers" who needed to be fought and to a "barbarism" of a kind that the United States had not seen for a long time. The White House later felt the need to apologize for the president's choice of words, which failed to take into account the negative connotations of the term "crusade" in the Muslim world.[33] However, this apology soon became little more than a footnote. The Bush administration was already on the warpath, and one was either with them or against them. With the machinery of war in high gear, the Bush administration made it clear that "bureaucratic impediments" would not be tolerated: "All the rules have changed," CIA director George Tenet put it. In a memo to his staff, Tenet directed them to fix problems "quickly and smartly." Allied governments and intelligence agencies were by no means to question the CIA or its conduct. Fast action was needed to win the war and "make our president and the American people proud." This opened the door for everything that followed—from secret torture prisons, to a dystopian surveillance state that spies on its own citizens to this day, to bombings of civilian populations whose victims are summarily declared "terrorists."[34]

While critics tend to focus on how the war was executed, they rarely question the war itself. Yet the fact remains that the Western invasion of Afghanistan was an illegal war of aggression. To this day, both the US intervention and the first ever invocation of NATO's *casus foederis* are still widely accepted as appropriate or even obvious responses to the September 11 attacks. But they were by no means so, and not only from the perspective of large swaths of the Afghan population. Though seldom acknowledged, the invasion of Afghanistan was just as unlawful as the subsequent invasion of Iraq. The persistent idea that Iraq was the "bad war" and Afghanistan the "good war" rests on flimsy justifications. These have only gained a veneer of legality and become part of political newspeak thanks to unilateral actions by institutions such as the UN. All references to NATO's *casus foederis* or the UN mandate aside, however, the United States was attacked not by another state but by several individuals from the terror group Al Qaeda. Not one of these individuals was an Afghan citizen. They had received flight training not in the Hindu Kush but in the United States.[35] Nevertheless, the Afghan people were collectively punished. Additionally, there had not been an "allied" government in Afghanistan that had "called for the support" of the Americans and their allies. Rather, the latter simply set one up after they invaded and gave it the reins of the state. The individuals who ran this government—which can hardly be described as anything other than a kleptocracy—massively enriched themselves under the protection of the West. From their perspective, the presence of NATO troops was simply a means of clinging to power. Furthermore, the invasion of Afghanistan was in no way a defensive act, as some politicians still try to portray it. Though the Taliban's brutal regime must not be whitewashed, they had nothing to do with the September 11 attacks. On the contrary, Al Qaeda leader Osama bin Laden wore out his welcome in Afghanistan in 1996 by declaring war on the United States from Afghan soil, an act that went against the interests of the Taliban. From then on, the Taliban wanted him out of the country as quickly as possible. They were in any case not the ones who had invited him to Afghanistan. Credit for that fell to the mujahideen warlord Rab Rasul Sayyaf, with whom the Americans would ally in 2001.

After September 11, the Taliban deputy prime minister Hajji Abdul Kabir offered to hand bin Laden over to the US in exchange only for evidence of his guilt. That's right: ironically it was the Taliban and not the "free world" that insisted on the rule of law.[36] The Bush administration refused to comply with this request. Instead it sought war, or rather, revenge for 9/11. "They must be killed," CIA's counterterrorism director Cofer Black said of bin Laden and his co-conspirators. "I want to see photos of their heads on pikes. I want bin Laden's head shipped back in a box filled with dry ice. I want to be able to show bin Laden's head to the president. I promised him I would do that."[37] After the fall of the Taliban, Washington rejected all peace offers from the defeated extremists, largely at the behest of Bush and Rumsfeld. Similarly, in the years that followed, Taliban leaders who were willing to negotiate were deliberately eliminated. In retrospect, this was a catastrophic miscalculation. Rather than make peace with the Taliban while they were still weak, the US paved the way for them to regroup. Eventually, the extremists experienced a massive rebound—and when the United States pulled out of Afghanistan in the summer of 2021, after two long decades, the Taliban recaptured the country almost instantly.

Political Dissent and Willing Accomplices

When it even existed at all, political resistance to the war was either not condoned or actively condemned. Not a single US senator voted against the Authorization for Use of Military Force. In the House of Representatives, the sole no vote came from Barbara Lee of California. "I do not want to see this spiral out of control. […] If we rush to launch a counterattack, we run too great a risk that women, children, and other non-combatants will be caught in the crossfire," Lee said at the time, warning of "an open-ended war" without an "exit strategy." Years later, Lee described the mood at the time in her autobiography. It was not easy for her to stand up to more than 400 other politicians in unanimous agreement with each other. Some of them attacked her afterward. Labeled a "traitor" and "terrorist sympathizer," Lee became the target of a defamation campaign. However, she stands by her decision to this day. As Lee writes, "This is the longest war fought in American history, and Congress never even debated whether we should go to war or not. That was precisely why I voted against that terrible resolution on September 14, 2001. It was extremely difficult being the only member of Congress to cast that vote, but that was the right vote and more and more members have told me so."[38]

The mood among the US's allies was similarly heated and unreflective in the immediate aftermath of September 11. On September 12, German chancellor Gerhard Schröder of the traditionally center-left Social Democratic Party of Germany (SPD) described the terrorist attacks as a "declaration of war against the entire civilized world," words that could have come from the mouth of Bush or Dick Cheney. What he said next would come to be repeated time and again in different variations—by Western heads of state and

Arab and Asian dictators alike: "We must now quickly resort to even more effective measures to eliminate global terrorism at its source. It must be made clear: those who aid or shelter terrorists violate all fundamental values of international coexistence."[39] In a subsequent speech, Schröder also emphasized that, "The struggle against terror will be a long one and demand from us great perseverance."[40] These words signaled Germany's entry into the War on Terror. Schröder was echoed by foreign minister Joschka Fischer of the socially liberal Green Party, who longed for the war in Afghanistan and rhapsodized about a "fight against evil." Other colleagues spoke of "democracy," "freedom," and an "implementation of peace" (*Durchsetzung des Friedens*).

The fact that the coalition government between the Social Democrats and the Greens enthusiastically welcomed the war while the conservative Christian Democratic Union (CDU), the libertarian Free Democratic Party (FDP), and the left-wing Party of Democratic Socialism (PDS, predecessor to the party Die Linke) formed the de facto "peace movement" seems all the more surprising in retrospect. "A government such as this one, a chancellor such as this one—they haven't earned our trust," the CDU politician Friedrich Merz argued, as hard as that is to imagine today. (The staunchly conservative Merz became the leader of the CDU in 2022.) Ultimately, 336 members of the Bundestag voted for and 326 against the war that was supposed to "defend German security in the Hindu Kush," as SPD defense minister Peter Struck described it one year later.[41] According to the German historian Gregor Schöllgen, the deployment of German troops to Afghanistan would have set off mass demonstrations and riots in the streets had there not been a coalition government between the SPD and the Greens.

A similar dynamic played itself out in other US allies and particularly in the UK under the leadership of Tony Blair and the Labour Party. In contrast to Schröder, Blair would again ally with Bush a few years later in the lead up to the Iraq War. From the Middle East to Central and South Asia, Bush and Blair are now viewed as brutal visages of American imperialism—under different political circumstances, both would probably be tried for war crimes at the International Criminal Court. This perception became particularly pronounced upon the death of Bush's secretary of defense Donald Rumsfeld in June 2021. Rumsfeld was among the most important architects of the War on Terror. He was an extremist who viewed wars of retribution against Afghanistan and Iraq as necessary and took for granted widespread arrests and torture as well as the murder of millions of people. The reactions to his death reflected these realities. "He has many Americans on his conscience, but above all hundreds of thousands of Iraqis" the German-Egyptian journalist Karim El-Gawhary commented.[42] The *Atlantic* described Rumsfeld as "America's worst secretary of defense" and a man who "never expressed a quiver of regret."[43] The journalist Jeremy Scahill referred to him as a "merciless war criminal" whose legacy should be viewed accordingly.[44]

Among Washington's most important allies in its War on Terror were numerous repressive Middle Eastern and Central Asian dictators whose brutality fed extremism in their regions. These despots stood to profit from the American war economy, and they saw an opportunity to further secure their power by participating in the war as willing accomplices. Many of them—such as Bashar al-Assad in Syria, Hosni Mubarak in Egypt, Emomali Rahmon in Tajikistan, and Pervez Musharaf in Pakistan—appropriated the Americans' anti-terror rhetoric and used it to attack political dissidents in their own countries. Afghanistan was virtually surrounded by the states these men led, and before the official deployment of American troops, CIA units were already operating there. This led to the accusation that the Taliban regime was training terrorists and providing them with shelter, which was said to make military intervention a necessity. Yet if they were to use this same logic, countless other states would be justified in attacking the US. Iran would have the right to attack the US for providing safe haven to the dictatorial king Mohammad Reza Pahlavi after he was deposed in 1979. So too would the many South American states where right-wing military putschists came to power thanks to the CIA and partners after having first perfected their torture methods in American military academies. It goes without saying that thoughts of this sort hardly occurred to any observers. Such ideas are still regarded as simply absurd or even taboo. In this way, one's own violence is constantly rationalized or even viewed as "good," as familiar doctrine continues to dominate: the United States is exceptional in every respect—and everyone must treat it that way. The fact that the US gets to determine who does and does not count as a "terrorist" is part and parcel of this doctrine. Back in September 2001, 21,000 US soldiers were already stationed in the region around Afghanistan. Within days after September 11, 12,000 additional troops were deployed to Central Asia.[45] Crucial support to this end was provided by post-Soviet Uzbekistan under Islom Karimov, another infamous dictator who exercised absolute rule. In Uzbekistan at the time, freedom of speech was nonexistent, and journalists and political dissidents were persecuted. According to the UN, murder was a part of everyday political life and was practiced in an "institutionalized, systematic and widespread manner."[46] Nevertheless, in 2002, shortly after the beginning of the War on Terror, Karimov's regime received $202 million as a thank-you from Washington.[47] Pakistan, which was ruled at the time by the military dictator Musharaf and regularly received billions in US aid, played a key role in escalating the War on Terror, with Islamabad even permitting drone strikes on Pakistani soil. Yet at the same time, Pakistan's establishment nexus of politicians, the military, and the ISI was playing its own game by either directly or indirectly providing terror leaders with shelter. The best example of this is Osama bin Laden himself, who was caught and killed by US soldiers not in Afghanistan but a secured Pakistani garrison city a decade after the September 11 attacks. In June 2020, Pakistan's prime minister, Imran Khan, even referred to bin Laden as a martyr during a speech in parliament.[48] The American crusade would have been logistically impossible without the help of Pakistan, Uzbekistan, and other neighbors of Afghanistan. Moscow also provided support for the American war in the very country where it had suffered a crushing defeat after a decade-long occupation. However, this was likely done with an eye towards strategically weakening the US empire by facilitating its entanglement in a "second Vietnam"—a scenario Moscow likely anticipated from its own experience in the Hindu Kush.

The Ideological Framework
of the War on Terror

OCTOBER 7, 2001, marked the beginning of Operation Enduring Freedom. Thousands of NATO soldiers invaded Afghanistan as bombs rained down across the country and the unmanned armed drone made its combat debut, forever changing modern warfare. Violence on this kind of scale required an ideological framework. A justification for the war was needed to placate the masses in Western states. This was especially the case given that the fall of the Soviet Union at the end of the 1980s had deprived the West of its longtime bogeyman and excuse for political aggression in the region. Ideological frameworks tend to be forged at the writer's desk, and a central component of the one that would support the War on Terror was the theory of the "clash of civilizations" proposed by Samuel P. Huntington in his eponymous essay from 1993. Three years later, Huntington went on to expand his essay into a book that divided the world into different "major civilizations" and argued that conflict was inevitable between these ostensibly rigid constructs.[49] In the process, Huntington committed a whole host of errors that have since been deconstructed by numerous critics.

The Indian economist and Nobel Prize recipient Amartya Sen,

for example, has illustrated that civilizations do not have fixed and rigid boundaries, making it difficult to categorize geographical regions according to them. Referring to his own homeland, which Huntington grouped within "Hindu civilization," Sen criticizes the neocolonial and Eurocentric approach, observing that India is a heterogenous country, home not only to Hindus but also Sikhs, Christians, and Muslims. The latter in particular, Sen argues, have played a crucial role in shaping virtually all spheres of Indian life and society often precisely because of their faith, yet they disappear in Huntington's account. Although Muslims are in the minority in India, Sen points out that there are still nearly 150 million of them in the country. This makes India one of the three largest Muslim countries in the world. Sen notes as well that individuals have multiple identities, a reality that Huntington's theory ignores. "The Islamic identity can be one of the identities the person regards as important (perhaps even crucial), but without thereby denying that there are other identities that may also be significant," Sen writes.[50] However, such subtleties and nuances are of no interest to the numerous devotees of the clash of civilizations, who prefer to continue believing that the so-called civilized world is at war with the "barbarians." This might be seen as an example of what is sometimes referred to as "othering."

In concrete terms, the concept of othering describes when a group of people are perceived of as "other" or "foreign" on the basis of some feature they have in common. This feature is used to continuously dehumanize them or even to justify violence against them in the worst cases. Narratives of this sort immediately took hold during the war in Afghanistan. Once again, the bearded, turban-wearing Muslim Afghan was stylized as a bogeyman by external aggressors, while his veiled wife was construed as in need of liberation. Such propaganda was welcomed by the Islamic extremist actors of Al Qaeda and similar groups for an obvious reason: the "conflict of civilizations" rhetoric also fits the narrative of the extremists on the "other side." Yet while Western discourses focus their critique on the latter, Westerners approach their own history remarkably uncritically.

This is of course nothing new. Many Western states have no desire to confront their present brutality or violent pasts. On this point, the Indian literature critic and author Pankaj Mishra has expressed particularly vehement criticism. Among other things, Mishra argues that the young men who left Europe to join ISIS were much more a product of European societies than those of the Middle East or North Africa. "Europe should view many of these young people who have chosen violence as part of a longer tradition of violence and dismemberment in Europe instead of blaming Islam or a particular part of the world. It's wrong to say, 'These people are bringing their problems to us.' These problems have played a central role in the modern world since its very beginning," Mishra told me in an interview in 2018 after his bestseller *Age of Anger* appeared in German. One of the preeminent critics of the War on Terror, Mishra has struck a nerve among a number Europeans and Americans. "The notion that ISIS represents something completely unknown and novel is actually quite an ahistorical notion. It is not a reflection of reality, for modern history has seen many assemblages of this kind. There have long been militant, extremist, and secessionist movements of young revolutionaries who sometimes simply wanted to blow themselves up in an exhibitionistic way. There have been men who celebrated violence as an aesthetic experience. This can be seen in numerous instances," he noted as we spoke.[51] In sum, the idea that ISIS or similar groups such as Al Qaeda are entirely without precedent is false, absurd, and another symptom of the historical ignorance and naïveté of Western societies. Many observers cannot handle Mishra's biting analysis.

I experienced this firsthand when the prominent German newspaper that had commissioned my interview with him suddenly lost interest in it. The responsible editor responded to the transcript with outrage, almost as if she felt personally attacked by Mishra's words. Apparently, it had stood her entire worldview on its head. Though the interview subsequently appeared in a different publication, reactions of this sort are hardly uncommon. This is not surprising given that many media outlets played a considerable role in laying the groundwork for the War on Terror by propagating the narratives that made it possible in the first place. Mishra himself speaks of an "intellectual-industrial complex" dedicated to formulating these narratives, one consisting of an extensive network with immense financial resources. Simply put, those who conform to the aforementioned lines of thought are rewarded. This discourse has spawned entire university centers, political institutes, think tanks, and various now-commonplace terms such as "Islamism" and "jihadism," which were neither overused nor carried negative connotations prior to 2001. Although these terms describe real problems within political and militant movements in the Muslim world, they have increasingly been degraded by sloganeering, deployed in a public debate in which they are seldom precisely defined. Similarly to the word "terrorism," they now seem to serve as a pretext for any manner of political decisions. Both Huntington's approach and the rhetoric of the War on Terror resonate within them. This is clear from the fact that no analogous terms exist for militant and extremist movements with Christian, Jewish, Buddhist, or Hindu roots. Obviously, the war-enforcement complex mentioned by Mishra played a major role in making these terms what they are today.

The media in particular acted as a kind of spearhead by beating the drums of war and firing up the masses for an invasion of Afghanistan. In addition to videos of Osama bin Laden and the collapsing Twin Towers, other images were omnipresent throughout the news: destruction in Kabul, menacing Afghan men with turbans and beards, Taliban extremists flogging women or destroying ancient cultural relics such as the Buddhas of Bamiyan. The numerous reports on Western television had an unambiguous message: "Look at this country where barbarism reigns. *We* must invade in order to civilize it." Afghanistan was portrayed as a country stuck in the dark ages. Military intervention would bring it into the light, liberate its women, and democratize its society. Yet though it may come as a surprise, this was not the first time Afghanistan was subjected to a hate campaign of this kind. Something similar had already occurred in the years prior—and some astute observers knew that they were about to experience déjà vu.

Other "Wars on Terror"

Time and again, it is forgotten that the Americans and their allies were not the first to invade Afghanistan. In fact, the country has been targeted by foreign occupiers on multiple occasions over the previous decades and centuries. During the nineteenth and twentieth centuries, the British Empire attempted to turn Afghanistan into a colony bordering British India as many as three times. Reports from that era hardly differ in their essence from contemporary ones. Just as they had done in numerous other places, the British gave free rein to their colonialist arrogance, their racism, and their Orientalist fairy tales in Afghanistan. They viewed the Afghan peoples as backward barbarians over whom the white man was entitled or even obligated to rule in order to bring them enlightenment. During their colonization attempts, the British allied with various Afghan rulers to advance their own interests.

Perhaps the most notorious of such rulers is the Afghan emir Shah Shuja Durrani, who took power in Kabul in 1803 with the help of the British Empire. In the First Anglo-Afghan War, local warlords supported Durrani, and the British fought the Afghan rebels who had declared a jihad against the king installed by non-Muslims. Durrani and his followers were eventually chased away to British India. Some prominent descendants of theirs can be found in India today, such as the actor Nasiruddin Shah, a relative of the warlord and Durrani ally Jan Fishan Khan.

The heroes of the Afghan resistance included figures such as Mohammad Akbar Khan, a son of Durrani's successor, Dost Mohammad Khan, and Mir Masjidi Khan, a native of the region of Kohistan to the north of Kabul. Medals of honor named after these men are now regularly awarded by the Afghan government, and during the latest occupation of the country, their recipients included US military members, NATO personnel, and foreign politicians. The irony here is that had Masjidi and Akbar lived two hundred years later, they probably would have been hunted down by US drones or imprisoned in some torture hell. Shah Shuja Durrani was an educated, eloquent man; he devoted himself to poetry among other pursuits and was typically praised by British chroniclers. However, he was also regarded as extremely cruel and psychologically disturbed. He would order even his own subordinates mutilated, castrated, or executed at the smallest mistake. Most Afghans view him as a national traitor, and the name Shah Shuja remains rather unpopular to this day. The scenarios that unfolded in the subsequent two Anglo-Afghan Wars were largely similar to those in the first. Afghanistan thus has a long history of being made into a pawn of various powers, and especially of the Russians and the British, who abused the country as part of their so-called Great Game.

Due to this history and the various trade routes that passed through Afghanistan, Kabul was already something of a cosmopolitan hub during the era of British colonialism. The capital was home to Muslims, Sikhs, Jews, Hindus, Armenian Christians, and members of various ethnic groups. The Kabul bazaar was a place where storytellers, clairvoyants, tailors, potters, blacksmiths, and merchants of all kinds would gather. Some of them peddled not only antique jewelry and goods from the Middle East and China but also uniforms and rifles that had been snatched up from British soldiers. This trend continues into the twenty-first century: at the so-called Bush Market in Kabul—named after George W. Bush—it is still possibly to purchase the boots or backpacks of US soldiers, or the ready-to-eat meals issued by the US military. Then and now, war in the country was the subject of literature and art. Just as Hollywood now produces action films about the Afghanistan War and the War on Terror, British authors such as Arthur Conan Doyle wrote novels about characters who underwent traumatic experiences in the Hindu Kush: Sherlock Holmes's partner, Dr. John Watson, is an Afghanistan veteran and traumatized war doctor who managed to escape the "savages."

At least according to his own account, Winston Churchill experienced the British war of colonization in Afghanistan up close and in person, and he was of the opinion that the crown stood no chance of success on this front. He had been convinced of this by men such as Mullah Sartor Faqir, also known as Mullah Mastan, a Pashtun tribal chief from the Valley of Swat in modern Pakistan and anti-colonial rebel whom the colonialists referred to as the "Mad Mullah." Some years back, the German news weekly *Der Spiegel* published a somewhat clumsy and Orientalist commemoration of this historical episode involving Churchill and the "Ur-Taliban."[52] Contemporary debates on colonialism have increasingly highlighted the fact that the subsequent prime minster of the United Kingdom, a man celebrated to this day in Western states as an antifascist war hero and political icon, held an extremely misanthropic and racist view of people from Africa and Asia, including of Afghans. Although some British colonialists found it in themselves to identify with Afghan peoples' "European facial features," Churchill was firmly of the opinion that they were "as degraded a race as any on the fringe of humanity" and lived in "squalid, loopholed hovels, amid dirt and ignorance." "Their wives and their womenkind generally, have no position but that of animals. They are freely bought and sold, and are not infrequently bartered for rifles. Truth is unknown among them," he claimed.[53]

In many societies of those countries that were colonized by the British, recent years have seen critical debates develop on Churchill and other actors of the British Empire. These debates have revealed the ugly visages of historical figures who continue to be glorified as heroes and idols in the West. Among others, the Indian scholar Priyamvada Gopal, professor of postcolonial studies at the University of Cambridge, has presented a scathing indictment of Churchill. As she has emphasized, from the perspective of numerous peoples who were oppressed by the British, Churchill was first and foremost a racist and mass murderer. The UK prime minister subscribed to misanthropic racial theories and praised the "Aryan stock" as a "stronger race, a higher-grade race." He also enthused about the "Anglo-Saxon superiority" of the British and white Americans and described anti-colonial dissidents as "savages armed with ideas."[54] Yet whoever brings up these facts is swiftly defamed and vilified. Gopal experienced this herself when a Churchill-critical university event in which she participated led to a brouhaha and attempts to "cancel" her. That being said, Churchill's racist worldview shocked even some of his supporters. "On the subject of India, Winston is not quite sane," Leopold Amery remarked. "I didn't see much difference between his outlook and Hitler's." Amery, the secretary of state for India and Burma during Churchill's war ministry, took particular issue with Churchill's stance on the 1943 Bengal famine, one of the most devastating famines in human history and a catastrophe that was effectively caused by the British. By refusing any and all food aid, Churchill consciously allowed hundreds of thousands to starve. Many Indians thus accuse him of genocide to this day. The Indian politician and author Shashi Tharoor has emphasized how the British colonialists' massive exploitation and mismanagement of Indian agriculture led to calamitous famines in Bengal and elsewhere. According to Tharoor, between 30 and 35 million Indians died during British colonial rule. In his book *Inglorious Empire*, Tharoor terms this mass murder of his compatriots "the British Colonial Holocaust" and questions why India and other states that suffered under the yoke of colonialism should have to subscribe to the Western view of Churchill.[55]

The British attempts to colonize Afghanistan found support in Germany as well. In 1858, the renowned German writer Theodor Fontane penned the following lines:

> We were thirteen thousand men,
> From Kabul our train began
> soldiers, leaders, wives, and children,
> Frozen, slain, betrayed.

> Our whole army has been scattered,
> All that's left strays through the night
> A God has granted me salvation,
> See if you can save the rest.[56]

Fontane's "Tragedy of Afghanistan" gives the impression that the British colonists were primarily the victims and not the aggressors in the Hindu Kush. The "betrayal" he mentions was the final assault of Mohammad Akbar Khan's troops, who attacked the remaining

British soldiers during their retreat and left only one man alive. Khan violated Islam's laws of war, which forbid attacking troops who have already surrendered. Indeed, the massacre stemmed less from religious fanaticism than a desire for revenge following the brutal British invasion of the country—something that neither Fontane nor other Western writers addressed, let alone condemned. The British and their local allies had regularly attacked civilians and committed unfathomable massacres, breaking into Afghan homes and assaulting women and children. From an Afghan perspective, expelling the British was an act of liberation, and Mohammad Akbar Khan's killing of the British colonial official William Hay Macnaghten is still commemorated in Afghan songs and poems to this day. Macnaghten was one of the faces of British colonial policy in the region and left behind a considerable amount of scorched earth in Afghanistan. Yet while the British may have failed in colonizing Afghanistan territorially, they succeeded in doing so ideologically.

Following their intervention, the worldview of Afghan elites became increasingly Western. Ideological constructs from Europe such as the idea of the nation-state, Western versions of modernity, and racist modes of thought such as biological racism were adopted and imitated, leading to additional suffering in the region. The events surrounding the British wars of aggression against Afghanistan exist in a continuum with the practices and the rhetoric of the War on Terror from 2001 onward. Analyses often mention that Western occupiers already invaded Afghanistan many decades ago and foundered. Many of the reasons why they were defeated in the past hardly differ from the contemporary ones. Marching headlong into a country about which they knew virtually nothing, they attempted to subordinate it to their own interests. They consistently ignored realities on the ground, but these realities eventually caught up with them. Meanwhile, the violence and brutality unleashed on the civilian population led to a backlash that ultimately resulted in defeat and retreat.

The British attempts at colonization were carried out not only by soldiers but also by journalists, Orientalists, anthropologists, and any number of other intellectuals who justified the war with their ideology. In fact, certain people continue to praise or relativize the Anglo-Afghan Wars today by spreading Orientalist fictions about the oppressed Afghans. The most prominent example of this can be seen in the work of the renowned British author and historian William Dalrymple, who has written several bestsellers for general audiences about the British colonial era. The Pakistani British historian Farrukh Husain, who himself has Afghan heritage, has accused Dalrymple of anti-Afghan racism and a neocolonial writing style that plays fast and loose with citing sources. In particular, Husain has criticized Dalrymple's Orientalist and sexist depiction of Afghan women, whom he accuses, among other things, of mutilating British soldiers. "Such writing insults all Afghan women. The reason for such allegations is of course to disguise the abuse that the British committed against Afghan women," writes Husain.[57] It is indeed astounding that Dalrymple focuses not only on "savage" Afghan men but also on the alleged violence of Afghan women. While his work forces them as well into the perpetrator role, it constitutes yet another instance in which the numerous instances of sexual abuse committed by British colonists go ignored.

The Genocidal War on Terror of the Soviets and their Afghan Allies

In his book *The Jakarta Method*, journalist Vincent Bevins addresses the mass murders in Indonesia during 1965 and 1966. Occurring in the context of the Cold War, these massacres primarily targeted leftist dissidents and claimed the lives of a million victims. Both supported and adapted by Washington, the Jakarta method was implemented multiple times in the following years in South America and elsewhere to destroy left-wing movements and replace them with right-wing, pro-Washington dictatorships. I picked up this book without any particular intention, but I had a vague idea of what to expect: like many other leftist authors, Bevins would probably condemn the American invasion of Afghanistan while playing down or completely ignoring the Soviet brutalities that had occurred merely years prior. Many representatives of the Western left process events according to the same predetermined template: from Chile, to Afghanistan, to Syria, the US is always the archenemy and source of all evil. The result of such "analyses" is frequently disastrous—and in Bevins's case, this quickly became clear.

The author produced superb work on Indonesia, but things became problematic as soon as he turned towards other states about which he apparently knew nothing. Of course, one can hardly talk about the Cold War without mentioning Afghanistan, and for Bevins, what unfolded there in the 1980s was obvious enough: the regime in Kabul was by all appearances progressive, democratic, and feminist, and it took up arms against the aggression of the US and its Muslim contras, the mujahideen rebels. The Red Army merely invaded to help an allied government and to catapult the country into modernity. This kind of rhetoric sounds familiar, doesn't it? Although Bevins mentions Afghanistan exactly twice in his book, he is convinced that the circumstances are unambiguous. He describes them using the dialectics of the Cold War. For him, what happened in Indonesia repeated itself in a slightly different guise in Afghanistan, with the Jakarta method being applied in Kabul as well: "In Afghanistan, where Soviet troops had been trying to prop up a communist ally for nine years, Moscow's forces retreated, the CIA-backed Islamist fundamentalists set up a fanatical theocracy, and the West stopped paying attention," he writes.[58]

Admittedly, the ability to present the events in Afghanistan in a manner so truncated might itself be regarded as a kind of art. Bevins is by no means alone in producing analyses of this kind. Over the years, I have had to hear and read them repeatedly. As soon as I have contradicted them, I have been vilified by people who have nothing to do with Afghanistan but do not appreciate having their worldview stood on its head. This worldview, it should be clear, is no less Eurocentric than that of the supporters of British colonialism or the intellectual architects of the American War on Terror. Some colleagues who view themselves as left-wing, anti-imperialist, and progressive have even refused to publish articles of mine in which

I have called out Soviet war crimes or made clear that the Afghan allies of Moscow were brutal torturers and war criminals. This sheer ignorance, which is still very present today, has produced many truncated analyses and at times even conspiracy myths that bear little to no relationship to the reality in Afghanistan under Soviet occupation.

A closer look at events makes clear that for the Afghan people, "America's longest war" was only one side of the coin. This designation, which has become widespread in the international media, is deeply America- and Eurocentric. After all, war and destruction have reigned in Afghanistan not for twenty years but more than forty.

Into the 1970s, Afghanistan was governed by its last king, Mohammad Zahir Shah. Shah came to power at a young age back in 1933 during a period of upheaval. He was an aristocratic ruler who lived and shaped his society accordingly. Nevertheless, it can be said in retrospect that Zahir's coronation marked the beginning of a long period of peace. "We were quite poor, but at least there wasn't war," many Afghans recall the era today. Yet things were far from perfect. While the Afghan aristocracy continued to plunder the country from its isolated bubble, poverty and hunger were rampant. According to Afghan fairy tales and legends, mountains, deserts, and other places remote from humans are inhabited by genies, giants, and any number of other mythical creatures. We might say that Kabul at the time was such a place, inhabited as it was by Zahir Shah and other elites who had nothing in common with the vast majority of the Afghan people. At the same time, a certain cosmopolitanism developed in the capital. Western tourists and many hippies in particular traveled to Afghanistan, which was advertised in travel brochures as an exotic country with unique cultural artifacts and excellent fruit. Meanwhile, a new generation of Afghans was coming of age—young people who longed for modernity and expressed this longing in various ways. In 1965, the king ventured to take the country a step forward, ushering in his "era of democracy" by clearing the way for the first parliamentary elections in Afghanistan's history.

Prime ministers advocating further steps towards democracy came to power. Though they were selected by the king, it should be recalled that many European states with parliamentary monarchies were not significantly more advanced at the time. Democratizing Afghanistan appeared possible, and entirely without Western intervention at that. After all, free elections and freedom of expression were not foreign concepts to the Afghans. Traditional tribal assemblies for forming a majority consensus had a history stretching back centuries. Freedom of expression manifested itself in various Kabul newspapers and all manner of other publications in the form of remarkably lively debates. On this point as well, it is useful to consider contemporaneous circumstances in Western states.

In West Germany in 1962, the so-called *Spiegel* affair saw critical journalists charged with treason for publishing an article about the country's military. "Our current goal should be the standard of that era," Masoud Qaane, an Afghan who has lived in exile in Germany for almost four decades, told me some time ago. "Today we know that the king took steps in the right direction. Now foreigners want to tell us what democracy means by rigging elections in our country." Like most of his relatives, Qaane fled Afghanistan due to the events following the "era of democracy." These events were the result of two fundamental mistakes by Zahir Shah that would seal his own fate and that of Afghanistan as a whole. First, he banned his own family members from politics, thereby ending the term of his cousin, Prime Minister Mohammad Daoud Khan. Second, he upheld the ban on parties, meaning that candidates who ran for parliament had to do so as individuals. Nevertheless, parties formed anyway. In 1965, a group of men composed of journalists, activists, and other intellectuals gathered in Kabul to found the People's Democratic Party of Afghanistan (PDPA), which initially claimed a vaguely Marxist orientation. Several years later, it would degenerate into a brutal Stalinism. Aside from the Communists, other actors included various Islamist currents. In spite of the tensions between the two camps, there were overlaps. Both sides were of the opinion that the "tyranny of the king" had to be ended, though one invoked Marx and Lenin and the other Muhammad. In many respects, the revolutionary rhetoric of the Islamists and Communists sounded similar. However, a third force beat them to toppling the government. While Zahir Shah was on vacation in Italy, his cousin Mohammad Daoud carried out a bloodless coup. The king was forced to remain in exile, and Daoud proclaimed the first Afghan republic.

Compared to the Islamists, Communist forces managed to profit from this move. At the time, the PDPA was already divided into two factions: the Parcham ("flag" or "banner"), which was composed of urban Afghans from various ethnic groups, and the Khalq ("masses"), which recruited mainly among rural Pashtuns. The Parchamis had already allied with Daoud and were able to take advantage of his coup. At the same time, Moscow continued to cooperate with Kabul, and numerous young Afghans spent time in the Soviet Union on scholarships. Whether Parchamis or Khalqis, most of them returned brainwashed. While the Khalq faction provided a significant portion of Daoud's military, PDPA leaders forged their ultimate plan to seize power. Leading the way behind the scenes was above all Hafizullah Amin, the right-hand man of party leader Noor Mohammad Taraki.

The son of a poor family of farmers in the Paghman District near Kabul, the charismatic Amin had directly experienced injustice and oppression at the hands of feudal landowners. After studying education in Kabul, he was admitted to Columbia University in New York. It was here of all places, at the very heart of capitalism, where Amin became a left-wing radical, at least according to his own definition. By the time he returned to Afghanistan in the 1960s and helped found the PDPA, he already had a long-term, "revolutionary" vision in mind, and he used his position as a university lecturer and teacher trainer to indoctrinate the younger generation with his ideas. Amin's mentor Taraki also worked as a teacher and was renowned as a journalist and author. He wrote a number of novellas in which he described rural Pashtun tribal life using Marxist dialectics. The Afghan historian Mohammad Hassan Kakar has described Taraki's writings as an imitation of the works of Maxim Gorky.[59] Whereas Taraki and Amin formed the leadership of the Khalq wing, the

Parchamis counted among their ranks leading ideologues such as Babrak Karmal, Mir Akbar Khyber, and the poet Sulaiman Layeq.

In the authoritarian Daoud years, Kabul increasingly became the site of tensions, intrigues, and plots. As the nationalist Daoud dredged up the Durand issue and called into question the country's border, Pakistan responded by drawing in Afghanistan's Islamists, who were unpopular in Afghan society at the time. In Pakistan, these Islamists were then trained to carry out a coup in Kabul and put an end to the Afghan nationalism that had become a thorn in Pakistan's side. The Islamists' eventual coup attempt failed miserably, and several of their ringleaders were arrested. Around the same time, Daoud fell out with the Soviet Union, which continued to pump billions into Afghanistan, and turned on his allies in the PDPA. A defining moment in this development occurred in April 1977, when Daoud defied Leonid Brezhnev during a meeting after the Soviet leader tried to tell him how he should guard his borders. "Afghanistan is not a Soviet republic," Daoud responded indignantly, departing from Moscow shortly thereafter. Yet the final straw came when Mir Akbar Khyber, a leader of the Parchamis, was murdered by unknown assailants on April 17, 1978. The Communists around Amin, Taraki, and Karmal—some of whom were in prison at the time—immediately blamed the Daoud government for the attack. Heavy protests by the PDPA ensued, leading to the so-called Saur Revolution on April 27. Named after the Afghan month in which it took place, this bloody coup carried out by the Communists was for many Afghans a brutal historical turning point. Thanks to the Communist presence within the army, the PDPA was able to seize power. Mohammad Daoud Khan was murdered along with almost his entire family—eighteen of his relatives in total—and Taraki's reign of terror began.

Declaring himself head of state, Taraki hunted down, tortured, and murdered all those who opposed the "revolution," including several of his own comrades in the Parcham faction. Although the PDPA described itself as "left-wing," "socialist," and "Marxist," most of its victims were the very people who are supposed to benefit from left-wing politics—workers, peasants, and students. A vulgar cult developed around Taraki. His supporters referred to him as the "great teacher," and even the Politburo in Moscow noticed that its ideological partner in Kabul was turning into a Stalinist extremist. Taraki promoted the so-called Red Terror, demanding the liquidation of anyone who resisted the revolution in any way. "Lenin taught us to be merciless towards the enemies of the revolution," Taraki told the Soviet ambassador in Kabul, Alexander Puzanov.[60] Left speechless by his conversation with Taraki, Puzanov suspected that Afghan society was going to be increasingly radicalized by the impending atrocities of the regime. In the following months, Taraki went on a rampage, arbitrarily torturing doctors, teachers, engineers, and other civilians. As the "great teacher" viewed Afghanistan's 30,000 traditional mullahs as a hindrance to "modern progress," many of them ended up in the dark torture dungeons of the intelligence agency and never again saw sunlight. In March 1979, Taraki perpetrated a brutal massacre in the city of Herat in western Afghanistan near the Iranian border in order to suppress an anti-Communist revolt. According to various estimates, Communist forces killed as many as 25,000 Afghan civilians in a matter of days. Several of the responsible parties were never called to answer for their crimes and still reside in Kabul to this day. Shahnawaz Tanai, the army commander who oversaw the atrocity, resided in Kabul until his death at age seventy-two in 2022. Taraki's reign of terror was taken over by his mentee Hafizullah Amin in October 1979, after the latter ordered him to be smothered with a pillow.

The machinations of the Afghan Communists have been described in great detail by Vasili Mitrokhin, a former KGB archivist. The files published by Mitrokhin reveal that leading Communists had been passing information to Moscow as far back as the Zahir Shah era. They also show that the Soviets supported the founding of the PDPA in 1965. Some PDPA protagonists went by aliases at the time, such as Taraki and Mohammad Najibullah, the last Communist president of Afghanistan and the former head of the infamous intelligence agency KHAD. While leading the KHAD in the early 1980s, Najibullah had countless people abducted, tortured, and killed. According to Mitrokhin's files and numerous eyewitness accounts, he even personally took part in many torture proceedings. Comparatively less has been confirmed about the precise nature of Amin's role. Unlike his comrades, Amin had neither a clear history as a Communist nor connections to Moscow. After taking power in Kabul, he went on such a rampage that the Politburo sought to get rid of him and even spread a rumor that he was a CIA asset. Given that Amin's mass torture and murder ended up provoking a Soviet intervention, it appears that some decision-makers in Moscow may have started to believe this rumor. According to some sources, Amin visited Moscow once in the mid-1960s. Though only a layover, the visit apparently radicalized him further.

Amin's reign came to an end when the Soviets launched a military intervention during Christmas of 1979. Amin was killed by a *Spetsnaz* unit and replaced by another dictator, the more controllable Babrak Karmal, who had previously left Kabul due to intra-party disputes. Protesting students in Kabul called Karmal a "second Shah Shuja," claiming that now the Russians, as opposed to the British, had installed a ruler to oppress the people. In its coverage of the Soviet invasion, the British *Sunday Times* wrote of the "tricks and terror in the KGB's Afghan duel." *Times* correspondent Anthony Mascarenhas, a Pakistani-British journalist who had helped to uncover the Pakistani genocide in Bangladesh several years prior, was the only Western correspondent on the scene. The horror of the Communist regime continued apace. Hundreds of thousands of people were forced to leave the country and became refugees. At the time, the Communists had already expelled or murdered large swaths of the educated population. In its propaganda, the regime spoke of a "fight against terrorism." The parallels to the War on Terror are readily apparent. Among other things, it was claimed that the Soviet Union had merely rushed to the aid of a supposedly progressive government involved in a "war against barbarity." In practice, the American War on Terror simply revived propaganda that had existed in the Hindu Kush long before 2001. As a consequence of the Red Army occupation, numerous Afghans joined the reactionary Islamist forces to fight the Soviets and the Kabul regime. At that time, it was common knowledge that the absolute majority of the war's victims were victims of the Soviets. According to a UN report from 1986, at least 33,000 Afghan civilians were killed between January and September 1985 alone, mainly by the Soviet army and their allies in Kabul. The report highlights that although several hundred civilians were also killed by rebel groups during the same period, this figure pales in comparison to the tens of thousands of victims claimed by the other side. It also foregrounds the fact that the Communist regime in Kabul and its supporters in Moscow intentionally used mass murder and mass torture against civilians.[61] These atrocities were committed above all in Afghanistan's rural regions, where mass graves from the time can still be found today, or in dystopian torture hells such as the Pol-e Charkhi prison in Kabul, which was massively expanded during the Soviet era to facilitate industrial mass murder. Murder, torture, and rape were part of the daily agenda in the dungeons of the Afghan Communists and their Soviet trainers. Many victims never reemerged from their cells, and to this day, family members regularly commemorate the dead by searching for their corpses.

In retrospect, it is striking that many left-wing or ostensibly critical analyses focus exclusively on the role of the CIA and Afghanistan's mujahideen resistance fighters, not to mention Al Qaeda and Osama bin Laden. Examinations of these actors are important and necessary to the discourse. Yet the erasure of Moscow's role is anything but helpful to the wider discussion. Rather, it clearly reveals racism, Orientalism, and anti-Muslim sentiment. Whereas suit-wearing torture bosses and mass murderers are ignored or even praised, the "bearded savages" are again labeled as essentially villainous. In this way, the Afghan resistance against the Soviet Union is usually completely dehumanized. Apparently, Westerners have a hard time standing in solidarity with a farmer or worker whose village was bombed by Russian helicopters if he prays five times a day. That said, one should not bloviate about American imperialism while ignoring the imperialist policies of other powers. How can it be that so many left-wing media outlets that hardly mentioned the Soviet invasion of Afghanistan, or even celebrated the invasion, criticized the US invasion in 2001? How can it be that left-wing students in major cities who protested against the brutal Vietnam War later sided with Afghanistan's occupiers? The renowned Irish-American journalist Alexander Cockburn, a man still regarded as a left-wing icon, once even wrote that Afghanistan "deserved rape" by the Soviets.

> We all have to go one day, but pray God let it not be over Afghanistan. An unspeakable country filled with unspeakable people, sheepshaggers and smugglers, who have furnished in their leisure hours some of the worst arts and crafts ever to penetrate the occidental world. I yield to none in my sympathy to those prostrate beneath the Russian jackboot, but if ever a country deserved rape it's Afghanistan. Nothing but mountains filled with bar-barous ethnics with views as medieval as their muskets, and unspeakably cruel too.[62]

Many may find it shocking to learn that such an unfathomably racist and misanthropic quotation came from a journalist who viewed himself as a progressive peace activist. In May 2021, I conducted a little survey where I posted Cockburn's words on social media and asked people to guess the speaker. Participants could choose one of four options: "European leftist," "European rightist," "British colonialist," or "American neoconservative." The absolute majority was convinced that the words could only have been uttered by a British colonialist in the nineteenth or early twentieth century (although various linguistic features already suggest that they couldn't have been all that old). Coming in second place were Washington's neoconservative politicians and ideologues, who have raised eyebrows with similar—though rarely so odious—quotations. Almost no one thought that the quotation in question might actually have come from by a leftist. When the American War on Terror began in Afghanistan two decades after Cockburn had penned the above words, he postured as an anti-imperialist opponent of the war. Suddenly, he was on the side of the very "barbarous ethnics" and "sheepshaggers" whom he once hated with such a passion. The reason for this change of allegiance is obvious. For Cockburn and many other left-wing observers in the West, Afghanistan and other countries in the region are simply ideological playing fields where they always confront their one true enemy: the United States. Meanwhile, they ignore that there was not one but two superpowers during the Cold War, both of which were capable of sowing tremendous destruction. By the end of the Soviet occupation, two million Afghans had died. Millions more had to flee their homeland, and entire generations were destroyed. Many young people had joined militant groups, not because the CIA had ordered them to but because they had lost family members in brutal massacres or the torture dungeons of the Kabul regime. In fact, the role of Washington and the CIA in Afghanistan during the Cold War continues to be overestimated or inflated to this day. Often it said that the Americans wanted to make Afghanistan the "Vietnam of the Soviets." According to some sources, the Afghan mujahideen rebels were already supported by American intelligence prior to the Soviet invasion. Whether or not this is true, however, is beside the point, for there was a different reason behind Moscow's military intervention: one sitting in Kabul and named Hafizullah Amin, the leader of the Moscow-allied PDPA government. Whereas there were virtually no links between the Afghan Communists' earlier coup and Washington, the same cannot be said of Moscow. It was the agents of Moscow who deliberately plunged Afghanistan into chaos. According to a former KHAD agent I interviewed under the condition of anonymity who held a leading position in the Afghan Communist intelligence agency at the end of the 1980s, Mir Akbar Khyber was murdered not by the Daoud regime but rather his comrade Babrak Karmal, who was already on the KGB's payroll at the time.[63] A resident of Germany for years, the ex-agent also claimed that actors within the party deliberately sought to bring about a violent revolution while Khyber stood in their way. Regarded as a moderate Marxist, Khyber was of the opinion that Afghan society was not ready for this kind of leap. Taraki, who declared himself president following the coup while escalating the situation, had also served as a KGB agent for years. While facts such as these are suppressed, many observers prefer to focus one-sidedly on Washington and its allies, Jimmy Carter's national security advisor Zbigniew Brzezinski, and Operation Cyclone. The latter was in fact the CIA's largest foreign operation at the time, yet this hardly changed the reality that it was Soviet violence that dominated on the battlefield. In 1980, the Carter administration provided the Afghan mujahideen with $30 million. Only in the subsequent years under Reagan did financial support for the rebels increase, eventually reaching $630 million in 1987. In the intervening years, hundreds of thousands of Afghans were killed as the mujahideen was left almost completely to its own devices. Further millions from Washington were pumped into the Soviet-Afghan war through the Pakistani intelligence agency ISI. However, the majority of rebels never saw this money, most of which went to line the pockets of corrupt mujahideen commanders. At the same time, the Communist regime in Kabul received billions in Soviet money and an enormous military apparatus that dwarfed that of the rebels. A closer look at Brzezinski and his role over the course of the war is also necessary.

The usual narrative—particularly among leftists—goes something like this: Carter's security advisor hated the Soviet Union because of his Polish roots and sought to wipe it out at any cost. Afghanistan seemed to him the perfect battlefield on which to hand the Soviets "their own Vietnam." Scholars such as the Irish historian Conor Tobin have already thoroughly deconstructed this narrative and made clear that Brzezinski's "Afghan trap" has little basis in reality. Tobin also criticizes the work of renowned journalists and particularly of historians who have spread and popularized theories such as this one in spite of a dearth of facts.[64] Often overshadowed by analyses of this sort is the reality that the Soviets and their Afghan allies waged a brutal war—a war on terror—which in many respects was no different from what would begin in the Hindu Kush some years later. Indeed, in the first days of their own intervention, the Americans even made use of Soviet war infrastructure. The best examples of this are the Bagram military base near Kabul, which was converted into one of the most infamous torture hells of the Afghan war; the Pul-e Charkhi prison; and last but not least the former personnel of the KHAD, the Communist regime's intelligence agency. "They were the best trained. They were actual intelligence officers," a CIA officer later said when justifying recruitment of ex-KHAD operatives.[65] Just how fatal this decision was will be revealed in the remainder of this book.

Excerpts from the Horror

IN MANY RESPECTS, the atrocities of the British and the Soviets recurred in twenty-first century Afghanistan. This time, however, the perpetrators were the NATO soldiers under US leadership who deployed in 2001 during the euphemistically named Operation Enduring Freedom. The following contains a detailed account of various war crimes committed by Western troops. All of the events described happened relatively recently. Because of their brutality, however, they have burned themselves into the collective memory of large swaths of Afghan society and will not soon be forgotten. They have led people in the regions where they occurred to come to view Western soldiers as brutal occupiers—which is precisely what these soldiers were. These events are also one reason why militant groups have won so many recruits in recent years, and why the Taliban ultimately managed to recapture Afghanistan once the Western occupiers withdrew. The crimes recounted here are merely a fragment of what has taken place in Afghanistan over the last two decades. All who are familiar with the situation on the ground know how difficult it remains to document civilian casualties. This difficulty stems not only from limited accessibility to the crime scenes but also from obvious political interests.

Since 2009, civilian casualties have mainly been documented by the United Nations Assistance Mission in Afghanistan (UNAMA). The annual UN reports published by this body count among the most important sources on the Afghanistan War. Yet although the work of the UN observers is obviously important and commendable, it has not gone without criticism. Although the UN is supposed to be an international institution, UNAMA is often accused of acting one-sidedly and in line with Western interests by those who maintain that NATO attacks—bombings, drone strikes, and special unit night raids—have killed far more civilians than have thus far been documented. It is true that most authors of the UN reports are based in Kabul or outside of Afghanistan as opposed to the regions hit hardest by the war. Criticism has also been leveled at the UNAMA for only starting to record casualties in 2009, even though the Afghanistan War began at the end of 2001.

In its first years, the war raged particularly fiercely—and cost a tremendous amount of human life. This was largely ignored, as any form of resistance or criticism was immediately suppressed in the early phase of the War on Terror. Furthermore, UNAMA's methodology has been called into question for requiring at least three different sources to confirm a single casualty, although journalists and human rights workers have very little presence in Afghanistan's most war-torn regions and the reporting from these regions leaves much to be desired. The true number of people killed in particular by drone attacks or elite special units in recent years remains unknown. An example of the latter can be seen in the crimes of SEAL Team 6. Although the soldiers of this elite Navy unit were responsible for hunting Osama bin Laden and other high-ranking targets, many of their victims were Afghan civilians. In March 2002, decked out in their official-issue skull-and-crossbones and crusader cross patches, they even attacked a convoy that was heading to a wedding party, murdering several passengers.[66]

Cases such as this one have usually been uncovered only through the painstaking efforts of investigative journalists who lacked any UN support. It is also noteworthy that the number of civilian casualties blamed on Western armed forces is always far lower than the number attributed to the Taliban, ISIS, or the Afghan army—almost as if to say, "Look at these Afghans killing each other while we stand by," the critics of these figures argue. Although the UN did help to illuminate events during the later years of the Afghanistan War, it must not be forgotten that it paved the way for this war in the first place by passing Resolution 1368 on September 12, 2001, and then completely abdicating its peacekeeping responsibility over the next several years. Its actions enabled the Bush administration and other warmongering governments to prosecute their criminal campaigns of vengeance unimpeded and unpunished.

The German Disgrace in Kunduz

In 2009, the German Bundeswehr colonel Georg Klein commanded American fighter jets to bomb two tanker trucks in Kunduz Province in northern Afghanistan. More than 150 Afghan civilians lost their lives as a result. This massacre marked a breaking point. The Germans in the Hindu Kush were not defending their own security but attacking that of the Afghans. The attack revealed that the Bundeswehr was directly involved in military activities and bore responsibility for the killing of civilians. There was no "clean" war against terrorism, not even for Germany, which had sent approximately 5,300 soldiers to Afghanistan at the time. Although the Kunduz affair constituted a war crime of the first order, the Bundeswehr long tried to play down the incident. Klein defended his order to kill by arguing the trucks constituted a potential danger for German soldiers. The vehicles had in fact been hijacked by Taliban soldiers on September 4, 2009, but the extremists quickly lost control of the gasoline-filled tankers and managed to get them stuck in a riverbed. Shortly thereafter, residents of the nearby villages began to approach and siphon off gasoline. Many of them were children.

There is no question that Klein committed a grievous error; even NATO concluded as much following an extensive investigation of the air strike. The colonel told the American bomber pilots that

NATO troops were engaged in combat with the enemy, reporting that the people gathered around the trucks were Taliban fighters. Both of these claims turned out to be false. In almost no time at all, Klein thus dehumanized the locals and declared open season on them. Following the atrocities of the British, the Soviets, and the Americans, the Germans too had now become war criminals in Afghanistan. However, the bombing has still never been properly investigated or confronted. Klein was even promoted in 2012, in spite of showing no remorse whatsoever for his severe mistake. The German Ministry of Defense tried to minimize Klein's promotion by burying it in a small notice on the third page of *Bundeswehr aktuell*, the military's internal weekly newspaper. Yet the news soon got around and made its way to Afghanistan.

For people in Kunduz, Klein's promotion added insult to injury. The families of the victims concluded that Westerners were being rewarded for murdering their relatives. What evidence did they have to the contrary? Imagine that an Afghan officer were to bomb 150 people in Bavaria or Baden-Württemberg and then be promoted instead of punished. Such hypotheticals are of course distant enough from reality that they are rarely posed, but they are useful for capturing the perspective of the people on the ground. In this context, it bears mentioning that compared to other NATO troops, the Germans were quite highly esteemed for some time in northern Afghanistan. They were viewed not as foreign occupiers per se but as people who genuinely wanted to help. There are historical reasons for this. A century ago, German engineers built infrastructure in Kabul and other provinces, and to this day, many Afghan peoples invoke their Indo-Germanic heritage and view the Germans as distant relatives. Both Persian and Pashto share a number of lexical and grammatical features with German. Yet the bombing of Kunduz and the handing of the incident by the Bundeswehr has left deep wounds that will be difficult to heal.

Karim Popal, an Afghan-German lawyer who represents the victims of Kunduz, has sharply criticized Klein's promotion as a slap in the face for the bereaved. As he has argued, it is incomprehensible to those who lost relatives in the air strike why a war criminal should be promoted to general instead of disciplined. Popal has also castigated the general manner in which German institutions have handled the Kunduz affair. Though the Bremen-based lawyer knew from the beginning that the legal battle against the Bundeswehr would be anything but easy, just exactly what lay before him became all too clear in 2010 when several prominent German media outlets launched a smear campaign against him. Among other things, they accused Popal of being a "Taliban lawyer" who was trying to take advantage of the victims in order to enrich himself.

Although the allegations were completely fabricated, Popal's reputation was permanently damaged. However, the Bremen lawyer—a man who had already spent years fighting for the rights of his compatriots, including in the area of asylum law—has refused to be intimidated. It also bears mentioning here that Popal is one of the few people who personally visited Kunduz after the air strike to conduct his own research. His struggle for just compensation for the bereaved continues to this day. According to reports, the Bundeswehr has paid $1.1 million in damages, more than half of which has gone to the survivors of Klein's attack. Meanwhile, each bereaved family has received all of $5,000—regardless of how many relatives lost. For other damages, such as destroyed cars, $10,000 were awarded. By way of comparison, relatives of fallen Bundeswehr soldiers receive around €100,000. For Popal, this makes a mockery of the Afghan victims, whose relatives do not even receive direct compensation: the German government's payments went through corrupt local politicians such as the governor of Kunduz and various other personnel on the ground who worked with NATO. Most of these payments vanished into the ether and thus effectively turned out to be a PR stunt. "Take the money and shut up" was the message. This is why Popal has taken it upon himself to secure higher compensation for the relatives of all victims. By demanding at least €39,000 for each of the victims of Klein's attack, he communicates to the world a simple message: Afghans are not cheap.

Popal's most recent lawsuit was dismissed by the Federal Court of Justice, Germany's highest court of civil and criminal jurisdiction, in 2016. Nevertheless, he continues to represent the victims from Kunduz and refuses to concede his legal battle. "We've given our own soldiers carte blanche at the international level and thus effectively suspended certain laws such as Paragraph 839 of the Federal Law Gazette (liability for breach of official duty). Suddenly, these laws no longer apply to measures taken abroad by the Ministry of Defense," Popal argues. Taken to its logical conclusion, this means that if the Ministry of Defense killed any person abroad for any reason, affected persons would not be able to file a lawsuit in Germany. This could create a legal precedent applying to all German soldiers on foreign deployments and preventing German war crimes from being classified as crimes at all. Perpetrators would continue to go unpunished. Like Klein, they might even receive promotions.

As a case study, the Kunduz affair presents the best illustration of how the German justice system has unambiguously transformed itself into an instrument of the government and the Bundeswehr, undermining its own independence in the process. *Der Spiegel* has issued a particularly damning assessment, asserting that "the *Bundeswehr* violated NATO rules, the minister of defense deceived the public, and the chancellor abdicated her political responsibility."[67] When it comes to war crimes, German courts serve political interests. Whoever speaks out against this status quo faces obstruction and harassment.

The more that Popal has made his demands public, the more intense the smear campaign against him has become. His lawsuit and criticism of the Bundeswehr's war in Afghanistan have made him many enemies in political and media circles. "It became clear that many media outlets were uncritically supporting the government narrative and were not prepared to report neutrally," he told me in conversation. At the same time, the completely powerless victims of the Kunduz bombing were silenced and erased. To this day, they remain little known among the German public. The fact that they have been ignored or completely dehumanized is all the more perfidious in light of how Klein has been portrayed in recent years as a "normal person" who made a "mistake." One of the victims from Kunduz was a twelve-year-old boy named Arif. He was one of the few people in his village who could read and write. For this reason, the other residents viewed him as a blessing. He often helped them write letters and managed to earn a bit of pocket money by doing so. Yet since that fateful day in September 2009, Arif can help them no longer. He was killed in Klein's attack.

For the killing of Arif and the other civilians who had gathered around the tanker, Klein has yet to be held accountable. The German office of the attorney general dropped an investigation against him in 2010.[68] No further criminal proceedings have been initiated. The German courts even ruled that Klein committed no mistake and acted in accordance with international law.[69] Meanwhile, Karim Popal and other lawyers continue to fight for the victims' rights. Recently, this fight was taken to the European Court of Human Rights in Strasbourg, where a 2020 hearing marked the first time that an Afghan bereaved in the war has testified. Abdul Hanan lost two sons in the attack—his eight-year-old, Nesarullah, and his twelve-year-old, Abdul Bayan. While the plaintiffs blamed Germany for killing both children, the lawyer of the German government claimed that the attack was carried out "on behalf of the United Nations." "The past twelve years have been an ordeal for my family and the families of the many other victims. We never received an official apology from the German government. All we want is for those responsible for the attack to be held accountable and to be adequately compensated," Abdul Hanan said. He emphasized that not only he but all of the affected families would continue to wait for justice.

According to Popal, Hanan's hearing was an important step. "It was a great success, but at the same time, it's still impossible to ignore that many Western states such as Germany or the United States have zero interest in the crimes committed by their troops," he said. His assessment proved right. In February 2021, the Strasbourg court issued a ruling that called on Germany to investigate the Kunduz bombing in accordance with legal standards, though Germany has yet to send either a Bundeswehr or independent fact-finding mission to Kunduz. However, the same ruling also claimed that Germany had not violated its obligations regarding an investigation. "For the Afghan village with dozens of civilian victims, today's decision is of course disappointing," the German human rights lawyer Wolfgang Kaleck, who represented Abdul Hanan in Strasbourg, summarized. In 2007, Kaleck and other lawyers founded the European Center for Constitutional and Human Rights (ECCHR), which is devoted both to the issue of Kunduz and other Western war crimes such as drone strikes against civilians. After the verdict was handed down, Kaleck said that the victims in Kunduz still hope for an official apology from the German government, which he also criticized for keeping numerous case files under lock and key. Popal, Kaleck, and other lawyers continue to accuse Klein of murder in accordance with Paragraph 211 of the German Penal Code or at least involuntary manslaughter in accordance with Paragraph 222.

An Overdue Confrontation with Australian War Crimes

In November 2020, an old bit of common knowledge was officially confirmed: Australian elite soldiers of the Special Air Service (SAS) had committed war crimes in Afghanistan, murdering at least thirty-nine civilians between 2005 and 2016. Hunting and murdering Afghans had been treated both as a kind of sport and an initiation ritual for newcomers. This perverse procedure was referred to as "blooding." A scandal also broke out over a photo taken during a party at a NATO base showing an Australian soldier drinking beer from what was ostensibly the prosthetic leg of a Taliban fighter. The picture made its rounds in both Western and Afghan media, causing widespread outrage. "May God punish these perpetrators." "How could our government allow such crimes to happen?" Comments such as these appeared en masse under the Facebook post of the Afghan outlet *Kabul News*.[70] The report by the Australian government accompanying the photo made clear that it did not depict an isolated incident. Reading like a log of horror, the report makes explicit time and again that Afghan lives were worthless in the eyes of Western soldiers.[71]

Many soldiers who were interviewed for the report claimed that killing Afghan civilians was routine in practice and "happened all the time."[72] Over the course of the investigation, which began in 2016, over 400 witnesses were questioned and at least fifty-five cases were opened against individuals. However, the biggest exposers of the war crimes were not state authorities but journalists from the Australian Broadcasting Corporation (ABC). These journalists were even targeted by the Australian security services. Rather than prosecute the soldiers who were in all likelihood guilty of the crimes of which they had been accused, the state focused instead on the journalists who had uncovered those crimes. The Australian police even raided editorial offices and confiscated hard drives. In Afghanistan, the Australian research team worked with Bilal Sarwary, a renowned Afghan journalist who accompanied them to sites in Uruzgan Province where SAS units had committed war crimes.[73] One of these sites was the village of Darwan, which was raided by Australian and Afghan soldiers one day in September 2012. Three civilians were killed in the process, in spite of repeated claims that the raid was simply a hunt for Taliban fighters. Later, the soldiers kidnapped several villagers, interrogating and torturing them over the following days in the very NATO base where the troops also held their raucous parties.

Exposés such as these caused the house of cards to collapse. In November 2020, the Australian military admitted on camera to the world that numerous war crimes had occurred in Afghanistan—a milestone in the West's confrontation with the Afghanistan War. Other states have regrettably not followed Australia's example and continue to remain silent.

Yet even Australia has a long way to go before all the facts come to light: SAS war crimes continue to be uncovered to this day, and not only by Australian journalists. For example, the American-Afghan journalist Ali Latifi has tracked down further victims of SAS units in Herat Province in western Afghanistan near the Iranian border.[74] One of them is Haji Abdul Baqi, who is originally from Uruzgan. Baqi will never forget what the Australian soldiers did to his family there. In June 2011, decked out in heavy gear and accompanied by attack dogs, they raided Baqi's village in the district of Chahār Chīnah. The pack attacked several men at the market, including many of Baqi's family members. When the dust had settled, four of them were dead: his brothers Saifulla and Bismillah and his cousins Mohammadulla and Juma Khan. Abdul Baqi's father, Abdul Hakim, died one year later of the wounds he had sustained from the soldiers and their dogs. Baqi, a merchant who now lives in Herat, emphasizes that zero military activity had occurred in his home village prior to the raid and that none of the victims was connected to the Taliban or other militant groups. Rather, the soldiers had merely lived out their sadistic fantasies, hunting and killing whomever they could find. After the fact, weapons were planted on dead civilians to justify the attack—a practice that is highlighted in the Australian report and appears to have been quite widespread.

According to the Australian journalist Soraya Lennie, who reported from Afghanistan from 2013 to 2016, abuses of this sort were commonplace. Yet although rumors of these and other war crimes circulate constantly, they have often been hard to prove. Such accusations have been leveled not only against Australian troops but also against the British, the Americans, and the Germans, as Lennie has noted. According to Sarwary, who took part in ABC's research, most of the victims and their families were farmers. Many of them were intentionally murdered so that they would not be able to speak out. Sarwary has also suggested that the extent of Australian crimes in the region likely far exceeds what has been discovered to date. "We still lack information about a number of things," Sarwary told me in conversation.[75] These reports are consistent with the most recent exposures relating to SAS war crimes, which are nowhere close to having been fully dealt with. In June 2021, ABC published a further exposé on a SAS massacre. According to multiple sources including members of the SAS unit in question, soldiers murdered at least ten Afghan civilians in Kandahar on December 15, 2012. Upon accidentally shooting a farmer, Australian soldiers carried out a systematic mass execution of all eyewitnesses of the incident, including a child. "They decided to kill all of them," an officer told ABC on condition of anonymity. The soldiers who were involved informed him of the massacre after they had returned to their base. "Honestly, it just sounded like a bit of a spree," he concluded. A video released by ABC shows one of the perpetrators, identified as "Soldier C," indiscriminately hunting Afghans with his dog. Eventually, he comes across an unarmed farmer. "You want me to drop this cunt?" the soldier screams before firing his weapon at point-blank range. The soldiers who witnessed the incident confirmed to ABC journalists that this was not Soldier C's first murder.[76]

The case of military sociologist Samantha Crompvoets illustrates how difficult it remains to confront SAS crimes. Crompvoets has interviewed numerous Afghanistan War veterans and has helped to drive the investigation into the Australian troops. Her work has not only led her to be criticized by the political and military establishment but also defamed and threatened. The Australian tabloid the *Daily Telegraph* launched a smear campaign against her. Prior to the release of her book *Blood Lust, Trust & Blame*, a critical look at the Australian Defense Force in light of the revelations of war crimes in Afghanistan, even Australian minister of defense Peter Dutton could not resist joining the pile-on, suggesting that Crompvoets's work posed a national security risk and threatening to cut her off from future government contracts for her research. The sociologist responded that she would not be silenced, emphasizing the urgency of confronting Australian war crimes in Afghanistan. Meanwhile, Dutton's characterization of the SAS massacres as a "distraction" makes it obvious that he has a fundamentally different view of the matter: "We want to get them back to business, concentrate on keeping our country safe and secure, not to be distracted by things that have happened in the past," Dutton has said.[77]

The Massacre of Kandahar

In July 2021, the Canadian journalist Murray Brewster published an article about the role of his country's military in Afghanistan. Murray's jargon resembled the British Orientalists and anthropologists who used to travel to Asian or African countries to write reports. Describing the Panjwayi District in the province of Kandahar in southern Afghanistan as a "wild, angry district," he gave the impression that the good Canadian military men were unsuccessful there because they were unable to subjugate the uncontrollable barbarians.[78] It is true that Panjwayi was crawling with Taliban fighters. Yet Murray failed to mention that the district was for years one of the grimmest theaters of the War on Terror. Western militaries regularly committed war crimes against the district's civilian population, literally driving them into the arms of the extremists. This was made especially clear on March 11, 2012, the date of one of the most gruesome war crimes committed in Afghanistan after the US invaded in October 2001.

One night, an American soldier by the name of Robert Bales left his camp and entered two nearby villages where farmers lived with their families. Bales proceeded to kill a combined sixteen villagers, most of whom were children, women, or elderly. The youngest victim was a two-year-old girl. Several of the corpses showed signs of having been burned. Apparently, the perpetrator had attempted to cover his tracks. In September 2013, a US military court sentenced Bales to life in prison. When Mohammad Wazir recounts that night of horror, his monotonous, serious tone does not waiver. A farmer from Panjwayi, Wazir lost eleven family members at the hands of Bales, including four daughters, his brother and sister-in-law, and their child. Visiting relatives in a neighboring village at the time of the attack, Wazir received the news via phone. His farm, which had once belonged to his great grandfather, had been completely destroyed. Afghanistan's southern provinces are famous for their pomegranates, juicy grapes, and giant melons—elements of a unique orchard. These are the fruits that Mohammad Wazir and his family had grown for generations, yet after the night of the massacre, virtually nothing of his fields remained. "I feel that I myself have been destroyed," Wazir said back in 2014. "I lost a reason to live and realized there is no justice. The Americans leave only destruction. But why? What have we done to them?" Wazir long ago gave up farming, leaving his home village after the night of the murders. As he has said, in the place where one has had everything taken, one has no reason to keep living. So he moved in with relatives in Spin Boldak, a town in another part of Kandahar. For every murdered member of his family, Wazir received $50,000 in compensation—American blood money that will not bring back any of the victims.

After the massacre, Afghan government officials investigated the crime scene, and an official hearing was held with relatives of the victims and witnesses from Panjwayi. Wazir and several village elders from the area were also invited to participate when President Hamid Karzai showed up with part of his staff. As Wazir spoke to them, he kept repeating one sentence: "Mr. President, we want justice." Karzai stared into the distance, likely knowing full well that he could not fulfill this wish of the victims' families. US military personnel in Afghanistan quickly began pushing the narrative of a lone actor, claiming that Robert Bales was a mentally unstable, traumatized, and sick man who had gone off the rails. The whole thing had been an isolated incident, they suggested. Wazir and the other villagers who were invited to the hearing did not believe this. One village elder asked Karzai why someone such as Bales would even be given a weapon and sent to a foreign country. No one could give him an answer. Yet Karzai had already lost faith in Washington at that point. The massacre in Kandahar, Karzai's home province, was certainly not the first with which he had been confronted.

The Afghan investigation team concluded that between fifteen and twenty soldiers must have been involved in the attack. The extent of the destruction would have been impossible otherwise. Additionally, the two affected villages were far apart from each other. "We are convinced that this would have been beyond a single person," research team member Lalay Hamidzai claimed. Hamidzai and his colleagues hypothesized that there had instead been two separate groups of soldiers that had attacked the villages. Karzai endorsed this version of events, also claiming that a lone actor would have been inconceivable. Bales's military base had already been associated with attacks against the Afghan civilian population. Between 2009 and 2010, soldiers who referred to themselves as "the Kill Team" had murdered at least three civilians in the adjacent Maiwand District. Moreover, it was revealed following the Massacre of Panjwayi that soldiers from Bales's base had used waterboarding and other methods to torture children. However, US investigators had no interest in any of this information and stuck to their theory of a lone actor. At the beginning of June 2013, the trial of Robert Bales began before a military tribunal—not in Kandahar but Seattle. This was in line with NATO's longstanding infringement on Afghan jurisdiction: in practice, Afghan courts have no authority over war crimes committed by foreign troops in Afghanistan, entirely regardless of whether civilians are killed in military raids, wedding parties are bombed by drones, or prisoners are tortured in Bagram. For the foreseeable future, American soldiers will also not end up before the International Criminal Court in The Hague, which is not recognized by the United States. Nevertheless, when the Bales trial entered its decisive phase in August 2013, several men from the village of Panjwayi—including Mohammad Wazir—were summoned to testify. For Wazir, this was quite significant. He resolved to speak from the heart and not hold back, for he had to relieve himself of the immense burden he had been carrying. But his plan was all for naught. The judge instructed Wazir that he was only to answer the questions posed to him by the state prosecutor or the defense attorney. Personal statements were not welcome. After the trial, some journalists tried and failed to interview Wazir and the other Afghan witnesses. Where the Afghans were housed during their stay in the US was kept secret.

Robert Bales, it is said, was a normal American. A native of Ohio, he was stationed in Iraq prior to his deployment to Afghanistan. He had suffered a head injury earlier in his military career, though why he became a mass murderer is not something the trial was able to explain. No psychiatric expert witness could provide an answer. Bales was sentenced to life in prison without the possibility of parole. He will probably die in a jail cell—yet indeed, only probably. In January 2021, Bales again made headlines by requesting a presidential pardon near the end of Donald Trump's time in office. For a brief moment, the American public was reminded of the former soldier's crimes. There was a real danger that Trump would pardon the murderer. After all, Trump did release multiple notorious war criminals over the course of his presidency in order to then brag about their actions and justify their "hunt for terrorists."

In November 2019, Trump pardoned the Navy SEAL platoon leader Eddie Gallagher, who murdered an Iraqi teenager apprehended on suspicion of ISIS membership in 2017. Gallagher posed next to the corpse of the victim after murdering the minor with a knife. His former colleagues have described him as "freaking evil" and "toxic," saying that he was "OK with killing anything that moved." Gallagher has also been accused of murdering a schoolgirl and an elderly man, though these allegations were never investigated.[79] Following his pardon, Gallagher has repeatedly thanked Trump and emphasized in interviews that he has no remorse for any of his actions given the necessity of the "war against the barbarians." Additional war criminals pardoned by Trump include four mercenaries of the infamous private military company Blackwater, who murdered fourteen civilians at an Iraqi market in 2007.[80]

Though Bales was ultimately denied a pardon, other war criminals championed his case. Particularly striking on this front was an opinion article by the Marine Corps lieutenant colonel David Gurfein demanding Bales's release and referring to the Afghan victims and their families as "terrorists." Gurfein even claimed that the US military conspired with the Taliban against Bales. "Army prosecutors befriended and teamed up with enemy combatants to testify against an American service member while our nation was at war—possibly a first in U.S. history," he writes. His article makes clear time and again just how present the dehumanization of Afghan war victims continues to be in the American debate. As "evidence" for the alleged terrorist affiliations of the witnesses, Gurfein mentions an ominous, unspecified "Taliban tattoo" worn by one and the fact that another had spent time in a US prison in Afghanistan—as if thousands of innocent Afghan men had not been detained, tortured, and abused by US soldiers over the course of the War on Terror.[81]

Meanwhile, Afghan observers have repeatedly claimed that massacres like the one in Kandahar were perpetrated far more than is generally known. The only reason that the Kandahar bloodbath could not be denied is that local journalists happened to arrive at the scene quickly. Yet this was not usually the case. During a 2010 raid in Paktia Province, US soldiers killed women and men in a village with zero connection to the Taliban. One of the men killed was even a police officer who had been trained by US troops. Eyewitnesses claim that US soldiers then used knives to dig their bullets out of the corpses—in front of surviving family members. The casualties included two pregnant woman and an underage girl. Although NATO claimed that the victims were Taliban, it officially admitted the true story after several US journalists including Jeremy Scahill had reported on the atrocities. This resembles what happened in the Massacre of Kandahar, when corpses were burned in an attempt to destroy evidence as survivors—including women and children—had to watch.

Prior to that incident, there had been other similar bloodbaths in Panjwayi Province. "In spite of the media coverage [of the Massacre of Kandahar], it was only one of several," a man from the region told me during a 2015 interview in Kabul. "In the deserts and mountains of this country, many horrible things have happened that the world will never know about," he mused. For his part, Mohammad Wazir has no desire to revisit that fateful night: "I've told my story so often, but each time it hurts all over again. I'm still waiting—just like everyone else from our village—for a just punishment for the perpetrators." At least when he stands before his creator, the farmer told me, the murderer will no longer be able to flee.

Only the Tip of the Iceberg

For many observers, journalists, and other experts on the Afghanistan War, the above examples are anything but surprising. In many Afghan villages, stories circulate about unreported incidents of NATO soldiers committing murder and torture. I myself have heard a number of brutal accounts that I have not been able to fully investigate. These include tales of the so-called Spin Taliban (Pashto for "White Taliban"), special US military units that would wear long beards and Afghan clothes and even speak Pashto while patrolling around wildly in a hunt for "terrorists." These units often attacked villages, stabbing and shooting innocent civilians. "They lured a farmer over and introduced themselves as Taliban members. After he said he had no problem with them, he was simply cut open," a man from southern Afghanistan told me several years ago. In 2013, the *New York Times* published a blog article about the White Taliban, which the author erroneously wrote off as the stuff of myths and legends. One possible reason for this is how difficult it is to report on such topics in a thorough manner. Virtually no sources exist apart from eyewitness testimonies.[82] Yet such testimonies are often simply dismissed.

The situation is similar with numerous other incidents that occurred in the shadow of the War on Terror, such as attacks carried out with new types of weapons systems or with the euphemistically named "Mother of All Bombs" (technically referred to as Massive Ordinance Air Blast, or MOAB), the US military's largest non-nuclear bomb. In April 2017, a MOAB was dropped on Achin District in Nangarhar Province, and the number of casualties is still unknown. For days after the detonation, the US military cordoned off the site of the crime. The Afghan government claimed that ISIS soldiers had been killed but never offered any proof. When I visited the affected region a few weeks later, residents told me that "many civilians" had been killed and that the perpetrators had already destroyed the evidence. For the military-industrial complex behind the development of such technologies of death, Afghanistan was a testing ground. The people living there—whether militants or civilians—were viewed as guinea pigs. "They test their weapons, and it's as if we're locked in a cage," a resident of the Khogyani District adjacent to Achin told me. "Some new kind of laser weapon was used here and destroyed an entire house," a friend of mine from the countryside in southeastern Khost Province told me as I was conducting research there during that same year. In light of the daily violence, my friend regarded that specific attack mostly as a footnote, and upon further investigation, I concluded that it had never once been reported. This triggered a feeling of déjà vu that would keep returning to me.

Over the course of my research, I encountered countless victims who had been almost entirely ignored. For this reason, they were typically surprised to be sought out by a journalist. In practice, the voices of these Afghans are only seen as worth something once their claims have been confirmed by Western actors. Otherwise, they are viewed as "not credible," "exaggerated," or "biased"—even when their accounts fit with those of war veterans who have come to criticize their missions. "Cases like the one of the Austrian special forces are just one small piece of the puzzle, which looks grim. We regularly shot at people whom we hadn't clearly identified. The Afghans who fought us, in my view justifiably, were completely dehumanized by us," the US soldier turned author Erik Edstrom has told me.[83] In 2020, Edstrom published *Un-American: A Soldier's Reckoning of Our Longest War*, an extremely critical account of his own mission in Afghanistan and of the War on Terror in general. During his year-long deployment in Kandahar in 2009, it occurred to Edstrom that the freedom and democracy people in the West take for granted was not actually being extended to the Afghans. Instead, they were being hunted, tortured, and murdered. This triggered a crisis of conscience for the soldier. In his book, Edstrom focuses on the mass killing of civilians while also attempting to understand how elements of the Afghan population became radicalized. "We started the war. We attacked and occupied their country. Who knows what I would have done if foreign powers invaded my country. I probably would have taken up arms too,"

Edstrom said when we spoke. He illustrates this point vividly in his book:

> [E]nvision that another country has violently occupied America in a preventive war to free you of America's current administration. The invasion is under the auspices of "fighting terrorism," and—not without lugubrious irony, seemingly lost on the invaders—they are systematically committing acts of "terrorism" under their own doctrinal definition of the word. Your home is searched by anxious, heavily armed young men aching to kill a "terrorist American." They are covered in angular armor pads, eyes obscured by black Oakley sunglasses. Your home is no longer a home—it's been dehumanized, called a "compound," "cache," or "built-up area." Your nation has been relieved of its sovereignty. You are no longer a person but reduced to a slur, akin to *enemy, insurgent, terrorist, sand nigger, Haji, towel head, goat fucker, cocksucker*, or the all-inclusive, multipurpose, good-for-every-occasion *motherfucker*.[84]

Edstrom shares the opinion that it will take years to uncover all of the West's war crimes in Afghanistan. The ex-soldier dedicated his book to the victims of the War on Terror he once believed in so strongly. Already on the first page, he mentions the more than 312,000 Afghan civilians killed by the United States and other countries over the course of the war. This figure represents a minimum estimate in need of constant updating. The real number of dead is probably far higher, possibly in the seven digits. Like many other Americans, Edstrom was intensely affected by the September 11 attacks. He came of age in the shadow of this event. "When you're still young, you get sucked in by the patriotic propaganda that's everywhere in the US, especially in pop culture," Edstrom told me. Though he joined the US military because he thought he had to defend his nation against terrorists, he now knows that his government's War on Terror in Afghanistan and elsewhere caused "more than one hundred 9/11s' worth of civilian death"—among a population that has long borne the brunt of American imperialist violence. "Two decades of the War on Terror have made it clear that our nation has fundamental problems and is destroying millions of lives with military interventions like those in Iraq and Afghanistan," Edstrom said. He is convinced that by repeating the phrase "never forget" exclusively to remember their own dead, Americans position themselves as eternal victims while playing down and ignoring their own violence. In fact, people in German, British, and Australian society do the same. When you are convinced of your own moral superiority, it is easy to fail to notice the monster you have become.

The question of confronting the War on Terror remains relevant in Germany as well. For in addition to the bombing of Kunduz, Germans may have committed other war crimes. In July 2014, the German television program *Monitor* reported on a Bundeswehr operation named Halmazag (Persian for "blitz") that killed at least twenty-seven civilians in northern Afghanistan near Kunduz during fall 2010. Among those interviewed was Ajmal, a teacher from the region who lost his son in the attacks: "One of the heavy projectiles hit the room, killing my son and badly wounding the rest of us." Whereas eyewitnesses claim that at least two other children were killed, the Bundeswehr continues to maintain that no civilians died in the four days of skirmishes.[85] Also especially troubling is the fact that elite soldiers of Germany's *Kommando Spezialkräfte* (KSK) were deployed in Afghanistan. Similar to the elite units of other countries, the KSK have been portrayed as heroes devoted to hunting down "terrorists."

A depiction of this sort can be seen in a 2020 documentary produced by the tabloid *Bild* titled "On a Secret Mission with the KSK: Hunting the Murderer of a Brother in Arms in Afghanistan."[86] However, this same unit has long been plagued by various scandals. It was even infiltrated by right-wing extremists during the 2010s. Though the KSK was partially "reformed" in 2020, a genuine confrontation with this development remains a long way off: numerous media outlets have described an "enormous problem with right-wing extremism" within the KSK that a handful of piecemeal reforms will not be able to eliminate. The fact that neo-Nazis had access to the resources of the Bundeswehr for years is an unparalleled scandal. One might assume that Germany would be better than the rest of the world in dealing with a scandal of this nature, but this has not proven to have been the case. Meanwhile, virtually no one has dared to pose the following question: to what extent were far right soldiers able to enact their misanthropic ideology in Afghanistan? Did they perhaps view themselves, like the Australians and Americans, as "modern crusaders" hunting "barbarians" in the Hindu Kush while their superiors turned a blind eye? The answers to such questions will be a long time coming. One can only hope that critical journalists and researchers will continue to ask questions that will drive a confrontation with the twenty-year war.[87]

The Six Greatest Failures of the War on Terror in Afghanistan

First Failure: Breeding Terrorism with Torture

ABOUT ONE HOUR outside of Kabul near the city of Bagram lies the eponymous former US military base. Bagram is the largest base the US established in the Hindu Kush. Prior to 2021, it served not only as the most important command center of the US invasion of Afghanistan but also as a military prison where torture occurred daily—a sort of Afghan Guantánamo, though probably much worse. In 2014, it came out that the US detention center at Guantánamo had been the site of not only torture but also murder. At least three inmates were allegedly killed in 2006 during CIA "interrogations"—read, torture. The deaths of these men, two Saudis and a Yemeni, were made to look like suicides by intelligence operatives, though a former guard later confirmed that suicide would have been effectively impossible. Also in 2014 came the CIA torture report (officially titled "Committee Study of the CIA's Detention and Interrogation Program: Findings and Conclusions"). This report focused not primarily on the torture camp in Guantánamo but rather on Bagram and other secret CIA prisons—so-called black sites. These prisons existed not only in Afghanistan but around the world, including in several European states such as Poland and Romania.[88] Most of the prisoners who did end up in Cuba were first locked up and interrogated in Afghan torture hell. As cynical as it sounds, a glimpse behind the curtains at Bagram almost makes Guantánamo look luxurious in comparison.

The history of Bagram Air Base spans decades. Its construction was initiated as early as the 1950s by the Soviets. Built by the Afghans with the help of their allies to the north, Bagram became Afghanistan's largest military airfield. Later, after the Red Army had invaded the Hindu Kush, Bagram served as an important Soviet base. Back then as well, it became the linchpin of interventionist oppression. Soviet combat helicopters regularly took off from Bagram to bomb Afghan villages while elite *Spetsnaz* units prepared themselves for brutal "anti-terror raids." To this day, Soviet veterans are involved in conflicts around the world. In 2021, it was revealed that mercenaries of the Wagner Group, a private military company based in Russia, had been contracted by Moscow to conduct "anti-terror missions" in Syria and other countries.[89] When the Americans launched their war several years later, the somewhat dilapidated Bagram practically stood ready and waiting—and was massively expanded. Already in the first years of the War on Terror, the base grew to the size of a small city. The apron of the air base alone now encompasses at least 130,000 square meters.

Over the course of the occupation, Bagram's infrastructure was specifically modified for American troops and their Afghan allies. Fitness centers and coffee shops sprung up on its grounds, as did American fast food chains such as Burger King and Kentucky Fried Chicken. Meanwhile, in the middle of this bizarre parallel universe, numerous people were held without charge and tortured, sometimes to death. For prisoners such as the Turkish-German Murat Kurnaz or the Mauritanian Mohamedou Ould Slahi, whose *Guantánamo Diary* was published while he was still interned in the detention center in Cuba, Bagram was the final stop before Guantánamo. Slahi's case demonstrates that not every person who moved in the milieu of the "Arab Afghans" can be viewed as a terrorist per se. After living in various countries including Germany, the Mauritanian joined the mujahideen in the early 1990s in order to fight the Communist regime in Kabul and its Soviet allies. He had been moved to act not only by the speeches of men such as Abdullah Azzam but by the various images of the war circulating throughout the media.

"I asked myself: how can there be such injustice, and why is no one doing anything about it?" Slahi recalled.[90] It was obvious to him that the Afghans were being oppressed and massacred because of their faith. Yet after Slahi had traveled to Afghanistan, he encountered a more complicated reality. Although the atrocities of the Soviets continued to make an impression on him, he also noticed the rampant corruption and leadership cults surrounding mujahideen commanders. His skepticism was confirmed after the Communist regime in Kabul had fallen in 1992 and various mujahideen groups began to fight each other: "I didn't want to be involved at all anymore. So I left Afghanistan and focused on my old life." Slahi, who had once led a modest existence, now wanted to support his poor family in Mauritania and help improve their standard of living. "Work hard and build a little house! (*Schaffe schaffe, Häusle baue!*) That was my plan," he told me, in the fluent Swabian he had acquired during his years in the German state of Baden-Württemberg. However, Slahi's plans were destroyed. His past caught up with him, and in 2002, he ended up via Bagram in Guantánamo. The reason for this can be summarized as follows:

Slahi had been with the wrong people (Arab mujahideen fighters, some of whom belonged to Al Qaeda) in the wrong place (Afghanistan and Pakistan) at the wrong time (early 1990s). One of his cousins had even become an advisor to Osama bin Laden. All of this and other unhappy coincidences were enough for the Americans to lock him up and torture him for fourteen years in violation of international law. In his book, the Mauritanian describes his ordeal in great detail. Among other things, he was sexually abused, force fed, and regularly beaten. In spite of these experiences, Slahi is an extremely positive and optimistic person. One reason for this is a man by the name of Brandon Neely, a former Guantánamo guard who befriended Slahi. Today, Neely counts among the most prominent critics of the torture prison and advocates for its closure. The fact that Guantánamo's gates remain open after two-plus decades of the War on Terror and four different presidential administrations is an unprecedented scandal. Yet while the US prison in Cuba has imprinted itself in public consciousness, Bagram is a different story. "Bagram was worse than Guantánamo. There were no rules there. After being there for three weeks, I was relieved when I heard I was being sent to Guantánamo," Slahi recalled.

Slahi's story is now known to the wider public after its recent adaptation into the Hollywood film *The Mauritanian*. One might refer to this as a kind of "positive propaganda," for pop culture can indeed be used constructively and educationally to reach those who might not be inclined to pick up Slahi's book or other critical literature on the War on Terror. *The Mauritanian* has helped continue a critical discussion about Guantánamo. Currently, thirty-nine prisoners remain in the cells of the Cuban prison, where around 800 people have been held for years without charge. All of them have been Muslim men. Those who have been released after years of torture have received neither compensation nor other forms of support, and many of the victims struggle with serious problems. The visibly aged Mohamedou Ould Slahi now lives in his homeland of Mauritania, yet his own government has denied him a passport, prompting criticism from Human Rights Watch in June 2019.[91] Critics have alleged that Slahi is intentionally being denied freedom of movement to prevent him from participating in political events and readings on other countries.

Most prisoners in Bagram were Afghans. Many remained nameless and unknown and had even less of a connection to terror groups than Mohamedou Ould Slahi. A striking example is Dilawar Yaqubi, a farmer and taxi driver from Khost Province in southeastern Afghanistan. In December 2002, Yaqubi was kidnapped and taken to Bagram along with three of his passengers. He had been arrested by a local militia that worked with the US military and the CIA, randomly hunting "terror suspects" to hand over to the Americans in exchange for large payments. In Bagram, Yaqubi was harassed and abused by soldiers. His shoulders were dislocated, and his legs were beaten to a pulp and then amputated. Yaqubi died after five days in Bagram. Two of his passengers, Abdul Rahim and Zakim Shah, endured a similar torture ordeal, though they managed to survive. They were then brought to Guantánamo in March 2003 before being released a year or so later.[92]

A documentary about Dilawar Yaqubi's murder, *Taxi to the Dark Side*, has been awarded an Oscar. Meanwhile, his family has yet to be given justice or any form of compensation. The German author Jürgen Todenhöfer has detailed a particularly brutal practice from Bagram. In his book *Du sollst nicht töten: Mein Traum vom Frieden* (*Thou Shalt Not Kill: My Dream of Peace*) Todenhöfer recounts the testimony of a man whom he refers to as Jack, a former US soldier. According to Jack, fighting dogs were used to rape prisoners in Bagram and extract all manner of confessions from them. "They'd even have said that they'd killed Kennedy without knowing who he was," Jack said. After the soldier witnessed one of these procedures, he left the US military and took a job at a private security firm. Although the practice recounted by Jack appears anything but unrealistic in view of the atrocities that have been exposed in Afghanistan, I wanted to follow up on the claim, as Jack is the only source named by Todenhöfer, himself a controversial writer whose work is considered untrustworthy by some. For this reason, I decided to track down an Afghan interpreter.

Afghan interpreters were present at the vast majority of "interrogations" performed by American soldiers. Recruited en masse at the beginning of the War on Terror, they were paid well for their work, unlike most other Afghans. They were also organized according to various ranks. There were men for simple debriefings and interviews with locals or Afghan security personnel, and there were men who would fan out with US Special Forces at night to hunt "terrorists" and conduct brutal raids. The latter often maintained close friendships with foreign soldiers and were viewed by them as an integral part of the team. They were also put to work in torture prisons such as Bagram, where they participated not infrequently in the interrogations. The Afghan interpreter industry is a complex topic. These helpers of the foreign soldiers continue to be hunted and murdered by the Taliban, who view them as traitors. A certain disdain towards them is also palpable, however, in wide swaths of Afghan society, including in the diaspora. For this reason, the US and its allies removed most interpreters—though not all—from of the country. In the southern US, it is even possible to find entire neighborhoods of Afghan interpreters. Usually following concrete threats, they received a visa or green card so that they could build a new life for themselves, far away from Afghanistan. Many of them now work as Uber drivers or food cart owners. Few talk about their former work, which they are banned from doing in any case by US authorities: their residence permits are tied to a non-disclosure agreement. Moreover, just as is the case with war veterans, many interpreters suffer from post-traumatic stress disorder. This issue has recently even found its way into American pop culture with the 2021 appearance of *United States of Al*, a sitcom that deals with the refugee experience of an Afghan interpreter. In the show, Awalmir, who goes by the nickname Al, is taken in by the family of a former elite US soldier, setting the stage for a charming and humorous clash of cultures. Immediately after the pilot episode, many Afghans criticized the vaguely effeminate depiction of Alwamir and the Orientalist manner in which he is taken in and introduced to American culture by his "strong" brother in arms. Yet many interpreters and other helpers have been abandoned by their Western employers entirely and remain in Afghanistan, where they continue to live in danger of the Taliban and other extremists. Often, bureaucratic hurdles stand in the way of their escape.

One aspect of the series that has not been criticized at all is that it never calls into question the work of the interpreters who collaborated with US armed forces and other NATO troops. "We've done bad things," a man in his late thirties told me. Mohammad, whose name I have changed for obvious reasons, now lives in the US. Prior to that, he spent years working as an interpreter for US Special Forces units that primarily operated in southeast Afghanistan. He also counts among those Afghan interpreters who were brought to the United States before they even submitted any kind of residency application themselves. Several years ago, Mohammad was in Kabul with his driver. Suddenly, his car was stopped by US soldiers. The driver was dragged from the vehicle and arrested. At first, the befuddled interpreter thought there had been some kind of misunderstanding. Shortly thereafter, an American colleague explained that the driver had been under surveillance for some time due to alleged connections to the Taliban. "My driver sold me out. He wanted to hand me over to them," Mohammad recalled. A few days later, Mohammad left Afghanistan with his wife and children. He continues to maintain friendly contact with his ex-colleagues, although he no longer expresses the same degree of pride in his former line of work. "A lot of interpreters were incompetent. They didn't have a strong command of the language, or they fed the Americans false information," he recounted. In many respects, the multilingualism and multiculturalism of Afghanistan was sorely underestimated by the West. Whereas many of the interpreters they hired spoke only Dari, the Afghan version of Persian, the main language in many regions of Afghanistan and especially those that were most affected by war is Pashto—the language spoken by the Pashtuns in numerous dialects. The Dutch Afghanistan veteran Nikko Norte pointed this out in an interview with the podcast *The Afghan Eye*.[93] Additionally, many translators were from urban areas and held contemptuous or racist views of people from the countryside, who often had different ethnic or tribal backgrounds. During our conversation, Mohammad did not want to address the question of whether he had participated in torture himself. However, he was not at all surprised by the statements of Jack, the soldier from Todenhöfer's book. "Things of this nature were commonplace there. Most of the perpetrators didn't see them as an issue. They thought that every prisoner was a terrorist anyway and deserved the 'punishment,'" Mohammad said. According to him, the detention center at Guantánamo must have been paradise island compared to the Afghan torture hells.

The complete CIA torture report has still yet to be released. Nine thousand pages remain under lock and key. As to whether they contain details of rapes committed with fighting dogs, one can only speculate. Yet the parts that have been published are already harrowing enough—with their numerous accounts of rectal forced feeding, solitary confinement in medieval dungeons, waterboarding, and psychological torture. On December 10, 2013, one day after the report's publication, control of the prison in Bagram was transferred to the Afghan government, though it is unlikely that this improved the situation in the cells. The army and military of Afghanistan's pro-Washington occupation government were known for their torture practices, some of which they learned from the CIA. At the beginning of 2021, Bagram Air Base was vacated by US troops during NATO's withdrawal from Afghanistan. International press coverage focused primarily on the soldiers and the growing strength of the Taliban as opposed to the atrocities that had been committed behind the walls of the base. That being said, the one can hardly be separated from the other.

A number of Afghans who spent the past years being tortured in Bagram or Guantánamo have now been radicalized. Many of them did not belong to an extremist group before their arrests but joined one upon being released. This was made obvious by the deal concluded between the Taliban and the US government at the end of February 2020. One of its clauses stipulated the release of several thousand prisoners from Bagram and elsewhere. Not all of these men had been members of the Taliban; quite a few had simply ended up on the release list thanks to the efforts of their relatives or fellow tribe members. Yet instead of heading home upon their release, many of them headed to the battlefield to seek vengeance against those Afghans who had once let them be imprisoned and tortured. A prominent and fatal example of this kind of radicalization is the case of the former Taliban commander and ex-Guantánamo inmate Mullah Abdul Rauf Khadim, one of the earliest protagonists of ISIS in Afghanistan. Khadim was considered a deputy ISIS governor in Afghanistan and is alleged to have recruited men on behalf of the self-proclaimed caliph Abu Bark al Baghdadi. He once belonged to the Taliban, but his arrest and torture radicalized him further. Following his release and return to Afghanistan, he swore allegiance to the newly emerging ISIS between 2014 and 2015. Outside of Afghanistan as well, ISIS must be viewed as a direct result of the War on Terror. Various leading ISIS figures from Iraq and Syria spent time in US custody, where they too were subjected to various atrocities by American soldiers. The ISIS caliph Baghdadi, who has now been killed, was a prisoner of the US in the infamous Camp Bucca near the Iraqi port city of Umm Qasr. It is there that Baghdadi met his subsequent predecessor, Abu Ibrahim al-Hashimi al-Quraishi, who led ISIS until killing himself by suicide bomb on February 3, 2022.[94]

The Afghan ISIS cell fought not only the Kabul government and the NATO troops but also the Taliban, who are classified as apostates within ISIS's *takfir* ideology. Mullah Khadim's own ISIS career came to an abrupt end in February 2015 when he and six other people were killed by an American drone strike in the southern Helmand Province. ISIS terror, however, remains present in Afghanistan. Recent years have seen devastating attacks that have cost the lives of hundreds. Above all, the terror group has targeted religious minorities such as Shia Muslims and Sikhs. This sectarian dimension of the conflict must likewise be viewed as an outgrowth of the War on Terror—an outgrowth that was in part cultivated in American torture hells.[95]

Second Failure: Crusader Culture

To this day, most Western troops who fought on the Afghan front over the last twenty years are portrayed as "the good guys." Whether British, American, or German, all of them were supposedly in the Hindu Kush to spread peace, freedom, and democracy. Questioning this narrative meant breaking a taboo. Whether in the United States,

Europe, or Australia, people did not want to cast doubt on the actions of their country's own soldiers. An emotional proximity to the soldiers existed from the beginning. It was maintained by politics and the media, as "embedded" journalists accompanied troops on the ground during their missions, or as bulletproof-vest-clad Western politicians visited NATO military bases in neocolonial fashion and recited platitudes to motivate the soldiers in their fight against the "barbarians." The United States boosted morale among its troops by sending over Hollywood stars and other celebrities to entertain them. Propagandistic measures such as these constantly insinuated to the Western world that everything was in order in Afghanistan—that there was simply a legitimate war going on against the last bastions of barbarity. In opposition to the Iraq War, the conflict in Afghanistan came to be held up as the "good war." Western war crimes that took place in the country over the last two decades were constantly played down, brushed off, ignored, or deliberately covered up. Those that did come to light were depicted as "unfortunate isolated incidents," their perpetrators portrayed as outliers among the rest of the soldiers. Yet over the twenty-year occupation, the facade progressively crumbled. Many Afghans who harbored no sympathies for the Taliban or other militant movements still cared little for foreign occupiers, whom they knew first and foremost as people who violently invaded their country to murder and torture. And indeed, many Western soldiers did not view Afghans as individuals who deserved to be treated as equals but as fair game to be shot down.

In Iraq and Afghanistan, many Western troops viewed them-selves as twenty-first century crusaders tasked with avenging attacks on "Western civilization." They deliberately hunted down Afghans and Iraqis to murder them, and they did not distinguish between armed fighters and civilians. In Western pop culture, they are mostly celebrated as heroes. A notorious example of this is the 2015 Hollywood film *American Sniper*, which tells the story of Chris Kyle, the "deadliest sniper in American history." During his time as a US soldier in Iraq, Kyle allegedly murdered 160 Iraqis, including women and children—an important aspect that is never shown in the film.

Instead, Kyle is portrayed as a hero and thoughtful family man who went to Iraq to fight nameless monsters in the name of democracy. Yet the Clint Eastwood-directed propaganda reel did not simply whitewash the figure of Kyle. Rather, it tried to justify the Iraq War by connecting the country to the September 11 attacks. In other words, Eastwood recycled the Iraq War lie for his audience—and did so successfully. *American Sniper* not only became a box office hit, it also elicited anti-Muslim resentment among viewers. In an open letter to Eastwood and lead actor Bradley Cooper, the American-Arab Anti-Discrimination Committee (ADC) alleged among other things that *American Sniper* had led to an increase in threats against American Muslims.[96] Yet at its heart, this troubling development was entirely in the interests of Chris Kyle.

In his bestselling book, Kyle made clear what he thought of Iraqis and Muslims: "Savage, despicable evil. That's what we were fighting in Iraq," Kyle writes. Kyle was fond of posing with his cross tattoo to show his Christian identity to the majority Muslim Iraqis. He enjoyed killing and wished only that he had killed more people in Iraq. "I loved what I did. […] I'm not lying or exaggerating to say it was fun. I had the time of my life being a SEAL," he wrote about his deployment. Kyle viewed himself as a modern crusader, welcoming the torture and murder of those whom he attacked. He was much less a pensive patriot than a mass murderer who was able to live out his fantasies in the Iraqi theater of war. Rather than even hint at questioning this side of the war, Clint Eastwood's propaganda reel completely erased it while stylizing Kyle as a hero.

In February 2013, Kyle was murdered by an Iraq War veteran suffering from post-traumatic stress disorder. Anyone who paid attention to the war knew that Kyle's was hardly an isolated case. The misanthropic warrior culture he embraced is widespread among Western soldiers.

Proud to Be "Kafir"

The theaters of the War on Terror were places where soldiers could experience this culture in the flesh. This often happened in an insidious manner that drew little to no attention from large swaths of the Western public. Yet a little internet digging reveals that for years, various anti-Muslim, racist, and far-right insignias in flagrant contravention of NATO norms and regulations were popular and widespread among soldiers in Afghanistan and elsewhere. These insignias could be purchased not only from small insider websites but also from well-known merchants who have worked with the US military for years. One particularly hot item was a patch depicting a cartoon medieval crusader with a ham hock and bearing the inscription "PORK EATING CRUSADER."[97] Also in high demand were patches and tattoos containing the word "infidel" or the characters for its Arab equivalent, *kafir*. Other well-known emblems included a cross with the word "Crusader," a turban-wearing person falling from a Muslim prayer rug accompanied by the inscription "HADJI DON'T SURF," and the profile of a Native American with the sentence "GOD WILL JUDGE OUR ENEMIES, WE'LL ARRANGE THE MEETING." The last two deserve special attention.

Hadji (usually spelled *hajji* in international contexts) is an honorific for practicing Muslims who have completed the hadj, the Islamic pilgrimage to Mecca. It thus hardly refers exclusively to members of militant Islamist groups. The same may be said of the turban-wearing figure, who is apparently being murdered during prayer. The depiction in question is thus explicitly anti-Muslim and declares open season on Iraqis, Afghans, and all other people targeted by the "crusade" of the Americans and their allies. The twenty years of occupation saw numerous attacks on Muslims who were praying in Mosques or outside. The victims were often read by soldiers or drone pilots as "enemy combatants" simply because they were engaged in the act of prayer. This kind of dehumanization has deep roots in American warrior culture, as the "Indian patch" makes clear. The figure it depicts is Geronimo, a chieftain of the Bedonkohe Apache who is viewed to this day as a hero by Native Americans due to his successful resistance against the cavalry troops of the white settler colonialists.

The fact that the perpetrators of the War on Terror viewed the contemporary theaters of war as a kind of Wild West 2.0 was also made clear when it came out that the CIA and the US military had referred to Osama bin Laden by the code name "Geronimo." The real Geronimo once had to hide from the US cavalry. Had he been alive today in the age of the War on Terror, he probably would have been hunted by drones and US Special Forces units such as the Navy SEALs. Many Native Americans, including Geronimo's great-great-grandson Harlyn Geronimo, were outraged when Osama bin Laden's code name became public. Yet many white Americans continue to view Geronimo as a "terrorist." From their point of view, the hunt for his scalp was justified, just like the hunt for bin Laden's head. This widespread subculture further raises the question of how seriously Western politicians and militaries should be taken when they bloviate about "winning hearts and minds" in Afghanistan and other majority Muslim countries.

Immunity for NATO War Criminals

In spite of the exposure of numerous war crimes, most Western politicians continued to stand by their soldiers. They often did so by assuming the role of colonial power in Kabul or Baghdad. This can be seen in the bilateral security treaty between NATO and the Afghan government from 2014. Hamid Karzai, who was in his last year in office at the time, refused to sign the agreement, making it clear that the task would fall to his successor. Washington, London, and Berlin reacted with outrage over the fact that the very man who they themselves had brought to power was now positioning himself against their treaty. Yet this treaty was in fact not a treaty among equals but a neocolonial pact that placed no value on the life of Afghans. Signed by Karzai's successor, Ashraf Ghani, immediately after his election, this agreement guaranteed permanent immunity for NATO soldiers in Afghanistan and made it clear that night raids, bombings, and drone operations would continue apace. In practice, it meant that notorious war criminals would have zero reason to ever fear punishment, as the Afghan justice system was not given a mandate to criminally prosecute them. Instead, this prerogative was left exclusively to the American occupiers themselves and their Western allies—and it is never exercised in the vast majority of cases. Pushing the treaty through was so important to the West that even German foreign minister Frank-Walter Steinmeier paid Karzai a visit in Kabul. Steinmeier practically forced Karzai to sign while also emphasizing that immunity for NATO soldiers was non-negotiable. Meanwhile, Karzai's refusal to agree to these terms was portrayed by *Spiegel* as simply an instance of "anti-American agitation."[98]

Several years later, Karzai told me that the immunity issue was one of the reasons why he had refused to sign the treaty. He had been convinced that most Afghans would view him as a "second Shah Shuja." The International Criminal Court in The Hague, which could presumably also pursue prosecution of those who committed war crimes in Afghanistan, is not recognized by the United States but rather treated as a mockery. During the Trump era, it was even threatened and sanctioned. Back in 2016, a report from the court claimed that US soldiers had probably committed war crimes in Afghanistan. According to prosecutors, there is a "reasonable basis" to believe that prisoners were tortured in Afghanistan over the course of the War on Terror and that torture also took place in secret CIA prisons in Poland, Lithuania, and Romania between 2003 and 2004. The report highlighted that both physical and psychological torture was employed, with prisoners being waterboarded, beaten, and raped. The court also concluded that the cases it described were hardly "the abuses of a few isolated individuals." Rather, these torture practices were implemented deliberately and systematically, on orders of the highest levels of leadership.

Yet the United States not only refuses to cooperate in bringing to light war crimes committed by its soldiers. It also actively blocks their prosecution: the so-called American Service-Members Protection

Act of 2002 shields members of the American government and military from criminal prosecution in The Hague. It even stipulates that US citizens and allies shall be defended against International Criminal Court investigations with force if necessary. According to the Obama administration, such investigations would be neither appropriate nor justified. Of course, however, the administration claimed to respect international law.

A harsher tone began emanating from the White House when Donald Trump assumed power in Washington. In September 2018, Trump's national security advisor John Bolton claimed that the International Criminal Court was "already dead to us." He railed against the employees of the court, threatening them with hefty sanctions and prosecution in the United States. In March 2020, the top prosecutor of The Hague approved an investigation into alleged war crimes and crimes against humanity in Afghanistan. Secretary of State Mike Pompeo immediately attacked the decision, calling it "reckless." He announced that the US government would respond by taking steps of its own to prevent American citizens from being made to appear before court. In March 2020, the Trump administration imposed economic sanctions and a ban on entry to the US against multiple leading representatives of the International Criminal Court. At the beginning of April 2021, these steps were reversed by Trump's successor, Joe Biden, yet the Biden administration underscored at the same time that Washington's stance towards The Hague remained fundamentally unchanged. "We continue to disagree strongly with the ICC's actions relating to the Afghanistan and Palestinian situations," a statement from Biden's secretary of state, Anthony Blinken, read. Several weeks prior, the court had announced plans to investigate crimes against humanity committed by the Israeli government against the Palestinian population. Israel, one of the US's most important allies, also refuses to recognize The Hague.

Third Failure: Warlordism, Corruption, and Pseudo-Democracy

During the occupation, Afghanistan's foreign ministry was situated in the Kabul "green zone," a secured area to which access was restricted. Private cars and taxis were not permitted to enter. Columns of armored cars and bulletproof SUVs were everywhere. Particularly popular were Toyota jeeps, which probably ate up more Western aid money over the 20 years of occupation than many a school and hospital. Soldiers, police officers, and other security personnel marched briskly back and forth. Visitors were frisked. On one street, behind thick concrete walls stood several palaces of the Afghan political elite. Most of these residences were guarded by small private armies that had served their respective power figures for years. Patronage has been completely normalized in Afghanistan. Whoever achieves an important position helps his relatives and tribe members above all else. At any rate, it is believed that your own kin can at least be trusted more than the crooks and thieves who mingle among the powerful. The same holds true in the house of Afghanistan's ex-president Hamid Karzai.

When you approach its outermost gate, a watchman immediately barks at you in Kandahari Pashto, the dialect of the Karzais. He is probably a Popalzai, a member of Karzai's tribe. This watchman is the first among many. He yells your name into a radio and then clears the way. Once you have passed through several more gates, subjected yourself to multiple extremely thorough friskings, and left your cell phone in the custody of a security guard, you reach a large courtyard completely enclosed by the complex. The whole time, you wonder how much it costs just to maintain this security apparatus.

You then encounter Sayed Ahmad Karimi, a young man in his mid-thirties with blue-green eyes and a clean-shaven visage. A secretary of the ex-president, he is tasked with leading visitors into a foyer in a building containing Karzai's office, his private library, guest rooms, dining rooms, and rooms for entertaining. The building also houses a private area for his family that is off limits to visitors. Karzai's residence is large, yet it too conforms to the usual Afghan traditions and customs. An important aspect of Afghan culture is *pardah* ("curtain"), or the separation of rooms for men and for women. In line with this custom, many Afghan houses contain specially furnished guest rooms with additional doors to prevent male visitors from seeing women residents. This form of gender segregation is typical in homes in many Muslim-majority countries. Yet the home of ex-president Karzai hardly suggests anything close to a typical family life. In spite of the fact that Karzai has not held any official office since 2014, the business of politics is a dominant presence behind his walls.

Karzai regularly hosts famous politicians, tribal representatives, former intelligence operatives, journalists, and foreign diplomats. These visits always follow a similar course: After leaving his guests waiting for some time, Karzai receives them warmly with open arms and leads them into his tea room or dining room. During a meal, the ex-president makes small talk, shares a smattering of anecdotes that have been repeated who knows how many times, and cracks the odd joke or two. Karzai's secretaries and other members of his former cabinet are present the whole time. Perhaps the most famous among them is the German-Afghan Rangeen Dadfar Spanta, who has served as Karzai's right-hand man since his days as president.

"Spanta, how's it going? Did you get a COVID vaccination in Germany?" Karzai asks his advisor during a lunch in February 2021. "No, unfortunately," Spanta answers. "The Afghan trick didn't work there." In other words, the kind of corruption that has typified Afghanistan since Karzai's time in office didn't work in Germany. "But the rule of law is a good thing," Spanta adds. Karzai nods in agreement. In a moment like this, even the most sober observer has to marvel at the surreality of the situation. After all, it was Karzai and his consorts who gutted the rule of law in Afghanistan, tolerating or even supporting all manner of corruption. In addition to the Karzai family, who counted among the largest beneficiaries of the plunder, the former mujahideen warlords became particularly rich off international aid. This culture of plunder was promoted by the CIA as early as the first days of the War on Terror, when agents carrying suitcases of cash appeared in Afghanistan and practically threw them at allied warlords and their militias. Since that time, however, a number of cash-filled suitcases have made their way out of the country.

In 2009, Ahmad Zia Massoud, the brother of the famous mujahideen commander Ahmad Shah Massoud and a former vice president of Karzai, was detained carrying $52 million in cash at the airport in Dubai. Although the responsible authorities knew that money laundering was underway, they let Massoud pass after a brief round of questioning.[99] This was by no means an isolated incident. For more than two decades now, the United Arab Emirates has served as both a tax haven and den of thieves for Afghan elites. Since 2001, over a trillion dollars have been pumped into Afghanistan. This astronomical sum could have been used to erect multiple cities in the style of Dubai with enough left over to build schools, hospitals, and all manner of infrastructure on every corner of the country. Most of the money instead made its way into the pockets of corrupt politicians and warlords. "Take the money, but invest it in Afghanistan," Karzai once appealed to a member of his government. Yet even this appeal, astoundingly ignorant and naïve as it was, was hardly followed by anyone. In Kabul, pompous villas and high-rise buildings sprung up in the shadow of slums and refugee camps that still lack basic necessities. Meanwhile, billions of dollars intended for Afghan widows, children, and farmers went towards foreign real estate or luxury goods. Many prominent members of the Kabul government took advantage of this system. Examples include the late warlord Mohammad Qasim Fahim, who was Karzai's first vice president, and Fahim's son Adib Ahmad, who worked for the Afghan intelligence agency NDS. Ahmad owns numerous properties in Dubai, as had his father. Fahim was also a partial owner of the Afghan airline Pamir Airways, which was accused of smuggling cash to Dubai. Fahim's uncle Haseen was a major shareholder of Kabul Bank, which collapsed in 2010 following a far-reaching credit scandal in which corrupt elites around Karzai were implicated. The protagonists of this scandal included Hamid Karzai's brother Mahmoud Karzai, who left his career as a restauranteur in the US and became a multimillionaire off Western aid money. Ghulam Farooq Wardak, another cabinet member of the Karzai administration, owns luxury real estate as well. One of his properties is located on Dubai's famous artificial palm-shaped archipelago, Palm Jumeirah, where various movie stars, celebrities, and billionaires from around the world reside part time. The Afghan ultra-rich also include Fatima Rabbani, daughter of the famous late mujahideen leader Burhanuddin Rabbani, who returned to Afghanistan at the start of the War on Terror and was murdered in 2011. Fatima Rabbani heads several business ventures in Dubai and is part owner of an Afghan restaurant. At least two other people from the circle of warlords around Karzai are also involved in the restaurant: Homaira Nasser-Zia, the daughter of Ahmad Zia Massoud of cash-filled suitcase fame, and Iman Nazeri from the famous Gailani family, whose members have moved in some of the highest political circles for years and held several important offices.[100] The corrupt warlords have also been courted by the German government, and several have even been treated on multiple occasions at the Bundeswehr hospital in Berlin. When Karzai's vice president Fahim was flown to Berlin for medical care in 2013, former Bundeswehr doctor and director of the NGO German Aid for Afghan Children Reinhard Erös remarked, "We send our soldiers down there to fight bad guys and build an at least somewhat democratic state. Then we use our tax dollars to pick up the hospital tab of one of the biggest war criminals in Afghanistan."[101]

All of these incidents represent merely a fraction of the corruption that took root in Afghanistan during the twenty-year occupation and was treated as completely normal by the responsible parties. Whoever holds a political position in Afghanistan has to be corrupt, or so goes the assumption of those who sowed the seeds of this culture. "That's just how politics works," they thought. Otherwise, what would be the point of holding higher office at all? Diplomats, ministers, attorney generals, and vice presidents are supposed to have enormous salaries—so what if they earn these salaries through criminal activity? As a result of this kind of thinking, the Afghan political apparatus built by the West was essentially a mafia network that maintained its own privileges by any means necessary. Far from promoting democratic institutions, the West primarily established a kleptocracy that drained the country of resources and was corrupt to the core.

Journalists who reported on corruption in Afghanistan were exposed to dangers and regularly threatened. When the British journalist Jessica Purkiss published an article at the end of 2019 about the machinations of the Kabul political elite in Dubai, she immediately received threats on Twitter. One came from Ahmad Zia Massoud's daughter Amina Zia Massoud, who raised the specter of legal action. To this day, however, none of what Purkiss wrote has been refuted. When the aforementioned restaurant of Rabbani, Massoud, and Nazeri announced its reopening in an Instagram post in 2021, I responded on the platform by drawing attention to Purkiss's exposé and the issue of corruption in Afghanistan more generally. I too was then threatened with legal action for "defamation." Those involved tried to influence my work as a journalist and intimidate me. Yet Afghan journalists who report on these machinations from within their own country face considerably greater danger. "We often receive threats, but we never know who sends them," Zaki Daryabi told me in the spring of 2021. Daryabi is the publisher of the renowned Afghan newspaper *Etilaat Roz*, which in recent years has made a name for itself particularly for its coverage of the issue of corruption—and its exposés on famous members of the Afghan government. Through leaks and investigative reporting, it has illustrated time and again how Western aid ends up in the pockets of corrupt politicians. Meanwhile, it has also made a number of enemies. The office of *Etilaat Roz* is located behind thick walls at a nondescript location in Kabul. Whoever enters the building is thoroughly frisked and questioned. At the beginning of 2021, Daryabi and his team received the annual Anti-Corruption Award from Transparency International, which has monitored Afghanistan's politicians for years and consistently ranked the country as one of the most corrupt in the world. "The prize has confirmed to us that we're doing something right. It encourages us to continue our work in spite of the dangerous circumstances," Daryabi said. For years, Afghanistan has been one of the world's most dangerous countries for journalists. During the last years many journalists and media workers were killed in Afghanistan. Though most of the perpetrators remain unknown, the murders can be traced back to the Taliban, ISIS, and even the highest circles of the occupation government and structures within the Afghan intelligence agency NDS.

How the Puppet Became Independent

Despite the numerous revelations of corruption, there have been zero consequences thus far for the exposed. The facts simply bounce off them. Hamid Karzai, the person who did more than anyone else to sow corruption in Afghanistan, is a good example of this. In recent conversations with me and other journalists, he has insisted that the Americans failed at their mission in the Hindu Kush. According to him, the corruption was only enabled by their billions in aid money. These two claims are not wrong, but they are also ironic coming from the mouth of a man who was a leading figurehead of precisely the system established by the Americans. One almost gets the impression that Karzai was an outsider the whole time with no influence over the various developments, or indeed, that he never held the office of the Afghan presidency at all. Yet this rigorous denial is part of the political strategy of Afghanistan's ex-president, someone who continues to present himself merely as a "concerned citizen" of the country as opposed to a political officeholder. Karzai once claimed to the Dutch journalist Bette Dam that he had no relationship with the CIA, even though the agency guided him through the early days of the War on Terror in Afghanistan and worked with Special Forces of the US military to help him take power. After she had continued her research and spoken with numerous eyewitnesses, friends, and allies of Karzai in Uruzgan, Karzai's political home in southern Afghanistan, Dam confronted Karzai again. "Do you know Graig?" she asked. Karzai hesitated briefly. Dam had done her homework, and he knew the charade couldn't last. "Graig, Graig is my best friend! How do you know him?" he replied, producing a photo of himself side by side with the ominous-looking CIA agent. "Graig," or Greg Vogle, was not just anyone. Rather, he was the CIA's station chief in Kabul. He and Karzai had already been in contact before the September 11 attacks. During the first US operations in Uruzgan, Vogle even saved Karzai's life.[102]

Karzai is a talented spinner of facts. This was made clear time and again during his trips abroad. In 2017, Karzai visited the quaint town of Schwerte in Germany's Ruhr region, the site of an annual conference on Afghanistan hosted by the *Evangelische Akademie Villigst*, an educational and cultural institution associated with the Protestant church. Karzai gives off a majestic aura, which the numerous Germans in the audience picked up on. His karakul hat, his cloak, and the way he waved as if he were friends with everybody not only made an impression but exerted a kind of gravitational pull on the attendees, filling them with awe. "Ha, my friend! Long time no see!" he called out to a German ex-diplomat in the first row. The man grinned sheepishly. Karzai then launched into a twenty-minute lecture about all manner of things—except the many failures from his time in office, as per usual. Most glaringly absent was any mention of the massive corruption or the participation of brutal perpetrators of crimes against humanity in his government. In the question-and-answer session following his talk, several guests raised these issues. What happened then was entirely predictable, at least for those fluent in Karzai's lingo. Corruption? All the Americans' fault. Brutal warlords? More like heroes of Afghan society who should be honored like veterans of the First or Second World War. Karzai also blamed the Western press for creating misunderstandings because of its antipathy towards Afghan politicians. Anyone who thought they had backed Karzai into a corner was proved wrong, for before the ex-president could be pinned down, he slipped away like a bar of soap. Deftly dodging the critical questions, he ultimately emerged as the winner, as charming and composed as ever. "Yes, unbelievable, isn't it? We also had no idea!" I heard him repeat multiple times after I had brought up various instances of malfeasance during his presidency. "In the end, one comes away thinking that Karzai isn't so bad," I was once told by a colleague, the Afghan journalist Abdul Rahman Lakanwal.

During Karzai's time in office, Lakanwal accompanied several tribal elders from Khost Province near Kabul to a demonstration against the latest US military operations in their villages. Once again, houses had been raided and innocent men kidnapped and taken to Bagram. Standing at the entrance of the Arg, the Afghan presidential palace, the gray-bearded men screamed at the security personnel, "We've come to have a word with that traitor to the people called Karzai. He lets the Americans kidnap, torture, and kill our sons." Suddenly, Karzai emerged. "Welcome, welcome. You must be tired," he greeted them. He proceeded to invite them into his banquet hall, where he delivered an impromptu history lecture. "The Pashtun tribes of Khost and Paktia fought with their heads held high against the British colonialists and for our independence," he said. The old men were flattered. After all, the president was speaking about their fathers and grandfathers. Later, they were provided with food and gifts. Each guest received a new turban. Once the elders had left Karzai's palace, Lakanwal asked them why they didn't tell Karzai off. "Karzai's not so bad," one of the men responded. "When it comes to the damn Americans, his hands are probably tied, too." This kind of "Karzai diplomacy" is famous in Afghanistan to this day.

In the spring of 2019, I confronted Karzai about the fact that even common people in cities such as Kabul and Mazar-e Sharif knew the details of his warlords' machinations. Specifically, I invoked the case of Atta Mohammad Noor, the former governor of the northern Balkh Province. After being ousted by Karzai's successor, Ashraf Ghani, Noor refused to go quietly. Instead, he took to Facebook, calling for an uprising via Facebook and ordering his militias to fight against other government troops in Mazar-e Sharif. "People talk a lot. I've never heard anything about this. Noor was a good governor," Karzai responded to me, though for once, he seemed to have some difficulty disguising his smirk. But in the end, Karzai's approach to public relations works. Even his critics ultimately pose for selfies with him, and they did so in Schwerte in 2017 as well. Yet Hamid Karzai is also underestimated by his former allies, who are de facto still paying for his residence and numerous security men and employees. At the start of the War on Terror, Karzai maintained good relations with the Bush administration. The situation in Washington changed when Barack Obama assumed power in the White House. The excesses at the Afghan presidential palace became an increasingly sore subject for the Americans. Motivated by international pressure, several US officials sought to look into corruption in Kabul more thoroughly. After having massively enriched themselves in the first years of the war, Karzai and his clan now feared that they would lose power and that Washington might turn off the money tap. The man who had taken power with Washington's help began to set out on his own.

The historian Alfred McCoy has compared Karzai's actions with those of the pro-American Vietnamese dictator Ngo Dinh Diem, who rigorously pursued his own interests during the Vietnam War while simultaneously counting on his backers in Washington. According to McCoy, the "ultimate weapon" of both Diem and Karzai was the "mixture of strength and weakness" with which they deftly manipulated their American allies. For a long time, the United States provided Diem with unconditional support in the form of weapons and money to wage war against the Vietcong, even as many of these resources were being used by Diem's brother Ngo Dinh Nhu to build a personal drug empire in greater Saigon. This presents a striking parallel to the Karzais. Before he was killed in 2011, one of the most powerful drug kingpins in Afghanistan—the so-called King of Kandahar—was Ahmad Walid Karzai, a half brother of Hamid Karzai. Following his death, it came out that he had been on the CIA's payroll for years.[103]

As time passed, however, the mood in Washington turned against the Karzais. Feeling the pressure, the president began to rail against the real holders of power in Kabul. And he knew how to score points in Afghanistan against the American occupiers. Suddenly, Karzai was speaking louder and more often than ever about the numerous civilians killed by US air attacks. He met with drone strike victims and hosted people whose homes had been raided by shadowy Special Forces units in the middle of the night. In 2013, he even issued a formal decree against these raids, which had killed mostly civilians. Even several of Karzai's own relatives in Kandahar counted among their victims. American politicians and military leaders were none too pleased that Washington's man in Kabul was now defying his "masters." The low point in their relationship occurred when Karzai refused to sign the bilateral security treaty with the US and NATO in 2014. Later that year, the Karzai era came to an end in what is often referred to as the first democratic transfer of power in Afghan history. In fact, however, no fair presidential elections have ever taken place in the Hindu Kush.

Pseudo-Democracy

For years, I have come across people of the opinion that it is impossible to democratize a country like Afghanistan. This has to do with the country's religion and culture, or so they argue. "The Afghans" need a dictator to keep them in line, they claim, as do other "backward" peoples in Africa and Asia. Views such as these paint the concept of democracy as essentially a Western privilege that does not function in practice everywhere in the world. Not only do I reject these views, I regard them as deeply racist and as a form of Orientalist obfuscation. For me, they above all testify to profound ignorance. More than forty years ago—before Daoud Khan's coup and the subsequent coup committed by Afghanistan's Communists—Afghans were intimately familiar with democracy and the positive effects it can have on society. During the "golden age of democracy" proclaimed by Afghanistan's last king, Mohammad Zahir Shah, in 1963, Afghans elected parliamentary represen- tatives for the first time. And in the decades and centuries prior, Afghanistan's social structures had already contained democratic elements. The best example of this is the *loya jirga*, Pashto for "great council," a multi-day forum where different peoples and religious groups convened to negotiate their concerns. Of course, the *loya jirga* was hardly a perfectly democratic institution. Yet in the eighteenth or nineteenth century, what institution was? Certainly none in Europe or the United States, where slavery, genocide, and later fascism were the order of the day. In the twenty-first century, the heirs to these traditions—the very Western powers that have not even confronted their own histories—tried to bring the Afghans democracy, and they could not have failed more miserably.

In the War on Terror, Karzai did not take power through elections. Rather, the man with the karakul hat was selected by the United States and catapulted to power along with his corrupt clientele. When elections were held in Afghanistan over the subsequent years to create a veneer of democratic order, Karzai twice emerged as the victor. In both cases, there were clear signs of widespread electoral fraud, yet rather than investigate, Washington, London, and Berlin let Karzai have his way. Instead of strengthening Afghan democracy, Karzai and his foreign allies thus consciously undermined it. As president, Karzai continued to be surrounded by his clique of warlords, who enriched themselves as the whole world watched. Various anecdotes from these days illustrate the extent of the corruption of Afghanistan's Western-installed elite. While the sons of famous warlords and politicians were dining at gourmet restaurants and indulging in any number of other luxuries in the United Arab Emirates or the US, NGO workers with the right connections to the presidential palace were getting rich off aid projects and building houses in the West with the money they had stolen.

This kind of kleptocracy did not end with the Karzai era. In 2014, Karzai's one-time finance minister Ashraf Ghani, a US-educated university professor and former World Bank employee, managed to take power following the presidential election. Yet Ghani was literally selected rather than elected—regardless of the fact that millions of Afghans had defied Taliban threats and put their lives on the line to go to the polls on Election Day. According to reports, turnout reached 58 percent, with seven million of Afghanistan's twelve million eligible voters participating.[104] Kabul saw an especially large number of people coming out to exercise their democratic right.

Ultimately, this was all for naught. When Ghani and his opponent Abdullah Abdullah disputed the results and violent clashes even started to occur between their respective supporters, US Secretary of State John Kerry intervened as many as three times before finally declaring Ghani the winner. Ghani thus officially won the runoff election, whereas Abdullah had been the victor in the first round. Far more than mere allegations of electoral fraud, however, there was clear evidence of improprieties. Ballots suddenly vanished. Employees of the ostensibly independent electoral commission appeared to accept bribes and act in the interest of the Ghani campaign. Yet the Kabul government's Western supporters had no desire to address such things, for they sought to present themselves as the enablers of Afghanistan's "first democratic transfer of power." Kerry's intervention led to the formation of a "national unity government" with Ghani as its president. Meanwhile, Abdullah was appointed chief executive or "CEO" of Afghanistan, a position with no basis in Afghanistan's constitution.

After taking power, Ghani drove the country into a series of political crises—although numerous observers had been hopeful when he took office. In contrast to Karzai and his clique, the former university professor's reputation was neither that of a drug kingpin, nor a warlord, nor a corrupt politician seeking to enrich himself and his family. Instead, he was viewed as an intellectual with the sophisticated solutions to deliver Afghanistan from its misery. And Ghani's academic background had afforded him some relevant experience—at least in theory. In 2008, he had published the book *Fixing Failed States: A Framework for Rebuilding a Fractured World*, which he co-wrote with the British political scientist Clare Lockhart. To the ears of many Afghans, the title of this book alone seemed to promise a miracle cure for Afghanistan, the failed state par excellence. After his election as president, he found himself in a position rarely afforded to a humanities scholar: a position that enabled him to put his theory into practice. Afghanistan became Ghani's experimental laboratory—and unfortunately his experiment failed miserably.

Rather than "fix" Afghanistan, he carried on the corruption of the Karzai regime, only with different protagonists. During the Karzai era, prominent warlords had occupied center stage. Now they were largely replaced by young, suit-wearing Afghans with zero political experience. The best example of this is the thirty-eight-year-old Hamdullah Mohib. During the 2014 campaign, Mohib had headed Ghani's social media team, and to widespread surprise, he was appointed to the coveted post of Afghanistan's ambassador in Washington once the new president was sworn in. In 2018, he became Ghani's national security advisor, replacing the far more experienced Hanif Atmar, who had allegedly fallen out with the egoistic Ghani. In spite of several diplomatic scandals, Ghani stood by Mohib, whom he had met during a lecture in London. Back then, Mohib was still working towards his degree in computer engineering. Mohib is typical of the kind of young men with whom the Afghan president would surround himself. Like Ghani himself, Mohib had studied in the West before returning to Afghanistan to "get to work." Yet Mohib and many of his colleagues knew little of the lived realities in Afghanistan. While in office, he could not even visit his native district of Khogyani in the eastern Nangahar Province, which by then had already been controlled by the Taliban for years. Other problems became apparent elsewhere in the Ghani administration, such as in the Ministry for Industry and Commerce, where several officials protested against their boss's modus operandi. Ajmal Ahmady, Afghanistan's minister of industry and one of Ghani's leading economic advisors, spoke neither Dari nor Pashto, the country's two administrative languages. He thus communicated with his employees exclusively in English, alienating them in the process. Ahmady subsequently served as the head of the Central Bank of Afghanistan (*Da Afghanistan Bank*), a position he received without the constitutionally necessary approval of the Afghan parliament. In one interview, Afghanistan's first lady, Rula Ghani, even suggested that the nomination of Ahmady and another person from Ghani's inner circle would be "pushed through with all means" as she defamed numerous members of parliament and described them as "personal interest representatives." Yet what the whole affair really laid bare was the presidential palace's own nepotism and thirst for power. Not only is Ajmal Ahmady considered a close confidant of Ashraf Ghani, he is also married to Ghani's niece, the US-Afghan Hannah Ghani. An exposé from 2021 made it clear that Hashmat Ghani, the president's brother and the father-in-law of Ahmady, managed to enrich himself and unlawfully obtain contracts with foreign firms thanks to large-scale corruption.

The Ghani family's wealth comes from a lucrative export business they have operated for over a century. Hashmat Ghani, who spent several years in the US and maintains close contact with famous figures of the American political establishment, now lives behind thick concrete walls in the Kabul district of Dar-ul-Aman. Here, one can find his luxurious villa and fleet of expensive classic cars. Ghani considers himself a philanthropist who wants to help his society. He also has a penchant for political theory. According to him, Afghanistan must proceed realistically, clearly define its interests, and pursue them above all else. Meanwhile, it should view Washington as a friend and partner that keeps its neighboring states in check. The brother of the former president hopes that such concerns will one day be championed by an Afghan-American lobby as well as by other important allies of the United States, such as Israel. Given these views, the fact that Hashmat Ghani has lived in Kabul for years and did not even travel to the United States to attend his own wife's funeral appears all the more paradoxical. An informant with whom I spoke on the condition of anonymity suggested that the chances that Ghani would face prosecution in the US are high. "He probably didn't pay his taxes. There's no other explanation," he told me. Hashmat Ghani does not like to talk about corruption or his outstanding taxes. As he describes it, his wealth is the product of his own hard work. In contrast to himself, he claims, his president brother is a bad businessman. "That's not an advantage in Afghanistan. A good businessman can lead this country," he told me back in 2017. Around the same time, Hashmat's son Sultan Ghani was flaunting his lavish lifestyle in Dubai and elsewhere on

Instagram. Family connections such as these hardly cast Ashraf Ghani in a positive light.

In 2019, several presidential elections followed one after the other in a chaotic series. Ghani emerged as the winner after several months, although the outcome was once again marred by accusations of electoral fraud and a conflict with Abdullah. Many observers foresaw a "John Kerry 2.0" scenario, expecting another intervention in the conflict by a US secretary of state, but the Trump administration was occupied with other matters. As the US special representative for Afghanistan Zalmay Khalilzad worked out a deal with the Taliban, the situation in Kabul reached the height of absurdity. In March 2020, both Ghani and Abdullah had themselves sworn in as president at two different locations. Each then issued a decree declaring the other an illegitimate head of state. In response, the United States cut a billion dollars in aid money for Afghanistan. Amid war with the Taliban and the COVID pandemic, the power struggle between Kabul's corrupt elites thus had direct economic consequences for millions of Afghans. The political crisis between Abdullah and Ghani finally came to an end in May, when Washington pressured both men into signing an accord stipulating that Ghani would continue to serve as president while Abdullah would lead the High Council for National Reconciliation. Yet the will of the Afghan voters, who turned out in much lower numbers for the 2019 elections, was once again ignored. Accusations of electoral fraud continue to this day. One of Ghani's most vehement critics is the American political scientist and Afghanistan expert Thomas H. Johnson. In an extensive report, Johnson wrote of Ghani's "fraud" and accused multiple institutions of involvement. Other critics have gone so far as to call the entire electoral process into question. According to the electoral commission, which has itself been accused of committing fraud in favor of Ghani, only about 1.9 million of the more than 9.6 million eligible Afghan voters—a mere 19 percent—even bothered to cast a ballot. Neither Ghani nor Abdullah thus enjoyed a mandate from the broad majority of Afghan society. Many people stayed home on Election Day not only due to Taliban threats but perhaps primarily because they had had enough of the corrupt Kabul elite's empty promises. The Ghani era also saw the continued promotion of warlordism. By far the most obvious example of this is the case of the brutal warlord Abdul Rashid Dostum, whom Ghani named his vice president after the 2014 election. In 2020, Ghani's government promoted the notorious war criminal general to the rank of marshal.

Fourth Failure: The Terrorism of "Angels of Death" and CIA Henchmen

Time and again over the course of the War on Terror, it was claimed that civilians were not under attack. Rather, the hunt was solely for terrorists and their leaders. In addition to Osama bin Laden, the Americans' most famous targets included the Taliban leader Mullah Mohammad Omar and the Al Qaeda vice emir Ayman az-Zawahiri. In order to hunt down these men, a novel, ostensibly precision weapon was deployed in the Afghanistan War for the first time: the armed drone. Piloted by remote teams, these killer machines were supposed to revolutionize how the United States went about pursuing its enemies. To this day, many people imagine drone strikes as flawless, Hollywood-style operations, with razor-sharp footage distinguishing civilians from armed fighters. At the push of a button, "Hellfire" missiles then eliminate the "bad guys." In this way, according to the narrative, terrorists are killed and innocent people are saved. This picture is not just distorted but entirely false. This was obvious as early as October 7, 2001, the very first day of the West's mission in Afghanistan. On this day in the southern Kandahar Province—the so-called Taliban stronghold—an armed drone was deployed for the first time in human history. Its target was none other than Mullah Omar himself, yet the Taliban leader was nowhere to be found. Just as is still the case today, the footage taken by the drones was hardly high resolution. Years later, it came out that drone pilots could neither distinguish children from adults nor militants with Kalashnikov rifles from miners with shovels. This prompted the US government to invent new terms to justify the killing. In 2012, it was revealed that the US had been officially defining all "military aged males" (or MAMs) near the site of a potential drone strike as "enemy combatants" per se. This was presumably the case on October 7 as well, when a drone operator spotted a house and a group of people and pushed the button. Several people were killed, though the Taliban leader was not among them.

The same scenario recurred constantly in the following years. Time and again, Omar, bin Laden, and other leading terrorists were pronounced dead following drone strikes—only to turn up later. Meanwhile, no one bothered asking who had actually been killed instead. According to the British human rights organization Reprieve, the pursuit of forty-one terrorists via armed drone led to the killings of as many as 1,147 civilians in Pakistan and Yemen between 2002 and 2014. Until Ayman az-Zawahiri's death by drone strike in 2022, American drones had failed to take out even a single famous target. Mullah Omar died a natural death in 2013, and Osama bin Laden was killed by an American Special Forces unit in 2011. The scenes of these two deaths are also worth noting. According to several reports, Omar died in the Zabul Province in southern Afghanistan near a US military base. Bin Laden was killed while hiding out neither in Afghanistan nor in the infamous Afghanistan-Pakistan border region but rather in the Pakistani garrison city of Abbottabad, approximately 135 miles away from Islamabad—a location crawling with Pakistani military and intelligence. Put simply, the Americans' two most important targets were not hiding in inaccessible mountain caves or remote villages. Rather, they had been living for years practically under the nose of the hunters. The many people hunted and murdered by Predator drones in their stead during the twenty-year War on Terror remain mostly unknown, both nameless and faceless. This owes in part to the fact that very few journalists bothered to report on the victims of the shadowy drone war. There are numerous reasons why this was the case. First, the nature of drone warfare is highly insidious. Due to its limited arsenal of weapons, a drone can only kill a limited number of people by means of a single attack. Thus, while there were numerous instances of the killer machines taking out small groups of agricultural workers or taxi drivers and their passengers, these instances were typically relegated to the margins of the news due to the small total number of dead, if they were even reported at all. Nevertheless, the broader picture is horrifying: according to the London-based Bureau of Investigative Journalism (BIJ), more than 13,000 drone strikes occurred between January 2015 and December 2019 alone, killing between 4,000 and 10,000 Afghans. Most of the victims were designated as "terrorists" or "terror suspects," adding dehumanization to death. Leading Western media outlets went along with this, including the *New York Times*, the *Washington Post*, and *Spiegel*.

In 2018, I conducted a quantitative content analysis of *Spiegel-Online*'s coverage of drone strikes, focusing primarily on the outlet's publicly accessible archive. Between September 1, 2001, and April 1, 2018, a search for "drone" generated 2,467 hits. Among these, 860 were articles that could be categorized and analyzed for my research. All in all, only thirteen results explicitly named civilian casualties of drone strikes.[105] In this context, critics and analysts have repeatedly noted that false reports from the drone war were extremely rarely amended. Once someone was labeled a "terrorist," that label stuck. Even when investigative journalists in the affected regions had proven that the victims had actually been civilians, corrections were not typically issued. One might thus justifiably speak of an "officials say" journalism that simply disseminated the statements of government bodies instead of critically questioning them. Many Western outlets practice this kind of journalism, serving as de facto PR departments of the CIA, the Pentagon, and so on.

This quickly occurred to me over the course of my work, which is why I increasingly came to focus on the US drone war's civilian casualties. The true extent of these casualties was unknown to me at the time. Yet the more I engaged with the topic, the clearer the abyss became. In 2014, the BIJ determined that Afghanistan has been drone bombed more than any other country in the world. Drone warfare came into public consciousness particularly during the presidency of Barack Obama. Under Obama, there was a tenfold increase in the number of drone strikes in Pakistan, Yemen, and

Somalia, countries where Washington had been prosecuting clandestine anti-terror wars. Obama even personally signed off on these attacks in weekly meetings where the so-called kill list was updated. In order to placate the American public, Obama mainly preferred drones and small Special Forces units. A remotely controlled, "safe" war looked better than the coffins of fallen US soldiers, as many as 100,000 of whom were present on the ground during parts of the Obama years—more than had been present at any other time. As all of these soldiers stationed in Afghanistan had little to show by way of success, Obama eventually reduced the "boots on the ground" and opted instead for ostensibly precise anti-terror operations, though these operations actually cost many civilian lives and further escalated the war.[106] Particularly in Germany, it must always be remembered that the drone strikes would not have been possible without data transmission through Ramstein Air Base, the infrastructural beating heart of the US military's illegal drone war.[107]

From the start of the War on Terror, the buzzing drones became a fact of daily life for numerous Afghans. They even left a cultural imprint, as is revealed by the various local names they were given. In Afghanistan and Pakistan, they are referred to in Pashto as "bungay" or "ghanghay," or as "Azrael"—the name of the angel of death in Islam. Over the course of my research, I personally sought out many drone victims. Some of them were Afghan civilians who are still struggling to survive, whereas others were young or even underage Taliban fighters who knew little of Islamist ideology and simply joined the militants to seek revenge. I encountered particularly tragic cases of drone victims who received neither justice nor any form of compensation for the crimes committed against them. One example was Aisha, a girl all of four years of age in 2013 when a Hellfire missile killed her family and severely disfigured her face. In yet another instance of innocent people being presumed to be "terrorists," her family's pickup truck was attacked by an American drone near the village of Gamber in Kunar Province. In total, fourteen were killed.

Aisha, the sole survivor, was transported to a French military hospital in Kabul for treatment. She received superior care there, yet her case was taken up by NATO, as news of her fate had already started to get around. The authorities wanted to cover up the entire war crime, for an Afghan girl having her face and family blown up by a supposedly precise killer machine would have been a PR disaster, exposing the grim everyday reality of the War on Terror. At one point in the hospital, a foreign woman approached Aisha's uncle Meya, foisting several documents on him and demanding his signature so that Aisha could receive treatment abroad. Meya was overwhelmed. A mason from Gamber who spoke no English, he himself had just been traumatized by the massacre of his family, and he did not want his niece to travel abroad with strangers. The woman told him that he could come with Aisha if he had a passport, but he did not, just like most Afghans. The following day, the unknown woman appeared once again and ordered him to sign. As Aisha's condition was worsening, he relented. Shortly thereafter, Aisha disappeared. When Meya tried to call the woman from the hospital several days later, it turned out the number she had given him did not exist. This marked the start of his search for his niece. He contacted Afghan politicians and Western embassies, but no one could tell him anything about Aisha's whereabouts. After months had gone by, he received a call from an unknown number. A man on the other end of the line explained to him in Pashto that Aisha was being treated in a hospital in Washington, DC, thanks to Solace for the Children, an American NGO that facilitates medical care for injured children from war-torn regions. The conversation left Meya convinced that Aisha was taken to the United States in order to hide her from the public eye.

According to her surviving family, they never consented to what happened to her. Against this version of the story, Solace for the Children founder Patsy Wilson claims to have received their full approval. She also alleges that the consent forms were signed by Aisha's grandfather, though her one surviving grandfather neither remembers meeting anyone nor signing any forms. Upon closer inspection, the role of Solace for the Children appears even more problematic. Specifically, rather than devote itself simply to providing humanitarian aid, the organization maintains close connections to a military and religious milieu consisting of Christian fundamentalists, war veterans, and military officers. Many children have come to the organization through the US military. Particularly dubious in light of this is the fact that Solace for the Children either suppresses or flat out denies the crimes committed by this very military. This was clear in Aisha's case as well. Among other things, Patsy Wilson even questions the very existence of the drone attack that wiped out her family and disfigured her face. "We do not necessarily believe Aisha was in a drone strike, but I know that is one of the stories," Wilson told the journalist May Jeong. "We have no facts. There are no facts," she claimed, adding that she has been told not to discuss details of the attack. She also refused to reveal how Solace for the Children came to Aisha in the first place.

In 2015, Aisha briefly returned to her family in Kunar in order to apply for a US visa. Jeong accompanied her on the journey, writing an in-depth piece about her and the drone war. Yet all things considered, the "faceless girl"—who now has successfully made it through numerous operations and speaks fluent English—remains largely unknown. Aisha's relatives in Kunar are convinced that the little girl was intentionally removed from the spotlight to legitimize the continuation of the war. "The Western armies supposedly wanted to liberate the women in our country. But in the end, they were the ones bombing, crippling, and murdering women and children," I was told in the spring of 2021 by an Afghan from Kunar who knows Aisha's family.[108]

"It's good that they're leaving"

In July 2016, the Obama administration published the first ever admission that the drone war had resulted in civilian casualties. According to the three-page paper, 473 drone strikes had taken place in Pakistan, Yemen, and Somalia between 2009 and 2015, killing between 64 and 116 civilians. Meanwhile, the administration claimed that the rest of the dead—between 2,372 and 2,581 people—had been exclusively "terrorist combatants." A number of observers of the drone war soon responded, noting correctly that even conservative estimates were far higher than the numbers released by the White House. They also criticized the Obama administration for failing to define "terrorist combatant" or to even mention Afghanistan, the world's most drone-bombed country. As a point of contrast: while in Afghanistan in 2017 on a two-month research trip, I was able to locate and confirm thirty civilian drone casualties who had been killed during Obama's time in office. Due to limited resources, my research focused solely on two provinces: Maidan Wardak near Kabul, and Khost in the southeastern part of the country. In Khost, I met Abdul Hadi, a young man whose father, Hajji Delay, was killed by a drone strike in May 2014. The drone team took aim at Delay's taxi cab and pressed the button, killing him and four passengers. Almost nothing remained of their bodies. Even the victims' bones had been reduced to dust and ash.

When I confronted Abdul Hadi with the figures from the US government, he responded as if he couldn't quite believe what he was hearing. "Do people in the West really believe such reports?" he asked, dumbstruck. Then he told me that hundreds had been killed by American drone strikes over the years in his native Khost Province alone. The victims' surviving relatives have received neither justice nor compensation to this day. However, this was not the case with all drone victims. In 2015, two Western NGO employees who had been taken hostage by Al Qaeda-affiliated extremists, an Italian by the name of Giovanni Lo Porto and an American named Warren Weinsten, were killed with their captors by an American drone stroke in the Pakistani region of Waziristan near the Afghan border. In the following year, it came out that Lo Porto's family had received $1.3 million in compensation from the US government. Several media outlets even reported that the compensation had totaled $3 million. The attack on Lo Porto and Weinstein received extensive international coverage. Barack Obama also released a statement expressing his regret and condolences. To this day, Lo Porto's family remains the first documented case of the family of a drone victim receiving financial compensation from the US government. Meanwhile, Abdul Hadi and other Afghan drone victims continue to wait in vain for compensation payments. Between 2015 and 2021, the US military spent a mere $2 million on compensation, most of which went to the families of people killed in US operations.

The amounts paid for victims have ranged between $40,000 and the laughably small sum of $131. In 2021, I paid Abdul Hadi another visit in Khost together with my colleague Mohammad Zaman, a local journalist. At the time, the pending withdrawal of the NATO troops had already been set. "It's good that they're going. They killed many Afghans, innocent men like my father," Abdul Hadi responded immediately when we brought up the withdrawal. He then told us that many people in Khost were still living in fear of drone strikes—that they have been traumatized and they panic as soon as they see or hear the unmanned aerial vehicles, even though drone strikes had sharply declined following Washington's February 2020 withdrawal deal with the Taliban. Available figures confirm that the frequency of drone strikes did in fact decline after that point. Shortly after Donald Trump entered the White House in 2017, the Obama administration's deadly drone war legacy was practically served to him on a silver platter. Under Trump, drone strikes increased around the world. In the first weeks of his presidency, they already increased at least tenfold. Subsequently, the American air war in Afghanistan also escalated. In 2018 alone, the US military dropped at least 7,362 bombs and rockets on the country—an all-time high at that point. Yet in the first months of the following year, this record would be broken. In 2019, at least 7,423 American strikes occurred, a rate of about twenty per day. This marks the peak amount of bombing experienced by Afghanistan at any point since the start of the War on Terror.[109]

The consequences of this escalation and the exact number of civilian casualties remains unknown. At the time, the Trump administration claimed to be "putting pressure on the Taliban" with the attacks, although most of the victims were civilians and not militants. In May 2021, it came out that at least 40 percent of all civilian casualties of US air strikes in Afghanistan between 2016 and 2020 had been children. In concrete terms, there had been 1,600 child victims. During the time period in question, at least 2,122 civilians were killed by these NATO attacks.[110] In 2020, a group of journalists investigating ten air strikes in Afghanistan between 2018 and 2019 determined that at least 150 civilians and 70 children had been killed. Contradicting many other "investigators"—such as the US government itself—the journalists actually visited the scenes of the strikes and compiled detailed accounts and facts. Just as had happened in the case of Abdul Hadi and other drone victims whom I've encountered over the years, surviving family members here reported that they had received neither an apology nor any kind of compensation. Instead, their murdered relatives were simply labeled "terrorists." In six of the ten cases, the US military continued to claim it had acted in self-defense, even after conducting its own investigations.[111]

"In Afghanistan, it is virtually impossible to distinguish between civilians and armed fighters. Anyone claiming otherwise is lying. We've been killing people for years without knowing their identities," Lisa Ling told me in March 2021. Ling knows what she is talking about. A former US Air Force technician, she was responsible for the maintenance of armed drones. Her main focus was on the very hardware installed on the unmanned aerial vehicles to help them locate targets with radio signals. Yet as the number of civilian casualties increased, Ling began to question both her work and the War on Terror as a whole. Eventually, she came to the following conclusion: "Our terror is just creating more terror." Since quitting the program, she has been active as a whistleblower and critic of her former employer. However, Ling carefully considers every public statement she makes, even seeking legal advice. Otherwise, she could easily be prosecuted by the US government as a "traitor" and end up in jail, as has happened with other whistleblowers. In July 2021, the whistleblower Daniel Hale was sentenced to forty-five months in prison for passing along documents pertaining to the drone war to the journalist Jeremy

Scahill. To Ling, drone strikes such as the one that annihilated Abdul Hadi's father, Hajji Delay, are hardly surprising. According to her, there were thousands of similar occurrences in Afghanistan during the two decades of occupation, not to mention in other countries upon which the War on Terror was visited.

According to Abdul Hadi and other Khost residents I've interviewed over the years, hundreds of drone strikes have occurred in the province. Like Abdul Hadi, many people throughout Afghanistan did not view the Americans and their allies as the "good guys" and welcomed their withdrawal. Yet even as the withdrawal was unfolding, this reality was neglected by Western reporting, which preferred to continue portraying NATO forces as would-be saviors who were simply overpowered by the "barbarians." Yet when one sees through the Orientalist and racist narratives that still dominate the discourse, it should hardly come as a surprise that the victims of the War on Terror had little sympathy for the American soldiers and their allies and instead viewed them as the primary cause of their suffering. "I really hope that we Afghans make peace with each other and that our country calms down," Abdul Hadi told me. He believes such a peace cannot be achieved with drones or bombs but rather only with genuine intra-Afghan dialogue and a diplomatic solution.

The Legacy of the CIA

Even during the final days of the American occupation, anyone who happened to be in Kabul would have noticed the presence of numerous military vehicles forming columns and aggressively speeding through the capital's gridlocked traffic. Heavily armed soldiers could be seen inside them, probably already thinking about their next deployment. The heavy SUVs bore the initials NDS, short for National Directorate of Security, the domestic Afghan intelligence agency built by the CIA after 2001. A de facto extension of the US intelligence agency that created it, NDS regularly terrorized the Afghan population. "They raided his house in the middle of the night and just took him," I was told by Mohammad Rahim, who requested that I not use his real name. One of Rahim's cousins who had himself served in the army was arrested without cause by NDS units in March 2021. Armed men had landed a helicopter on the roof of his family's home before forcing their way in and kidnapping him. Following the incident, his family moved out of their Kabul district in fear. "Why are innocent people just being kidnapped? We're all worried and haven't been able to contact my cousin since," Rahim said. A similar operation on January 5, 2020, ended in a massacre. Around 7:30 that evening, NDS units raided a house in a famous Kabul district. A few hours later, five people were dead. "They attacked our house in an extremely brutal way, leaving a bloodbath," one of the eyewitnesses later told me. Among the dead was a man named Amer Abdul Sattar, a famous mujahideen commander who had fought the Soviets in the 1980s and been an important ally of the Afghan president Ashraf Ghani for some time. Sattar was from Parwan Province to the north of Kabul and had been staying with friends in the capital on the weekend when the attack occurred. "Sattar and his son were our guests. They were murdered along with my father and brother," I was told by Shafi Ghorbandi, the son of the murdered host. All evidence suggested that Sattar had been the target of the NDS raid. Even his son was murdered by the special units. Yet the question of why a political ally of Afghanistan's president had become a target of the latter's own intelligence agency remained unanswered. Shortly after the raid, Sattar's family was received by Ghani in the Arg, Afghanistan's presidential palace, and the president promised an investigation into the massacre. At the same time, the NDS attack in Ghorbandi's house also became the subject of an intense debate in parliament. Several members of parliament demanded not only an investigation to the case of Sattar but also the other brutal raids that had taken place in Afghanistan. In one of these raids that had occurred in the same month in a village in Laghman Province, the secret units had killed an elderly man and kidnapped his four sons. These units belonged to a virtually impenetrable counterterrorism network that the CIA had installed throughout the country.

Over the two decades of the occupation, the CIA constructed a massive intra-Afghan security and surveillance apparatus. The agency had stations at several locations in the country, including in Kabul, at Jalalabad Airport in the east, and in the city of Khost in the southeast. Spy balloons dotted the sky, creating a dystopian atmosphere that eventually became a normal part of life. The NDS commanded numerous shadowy paramilitary units that regularly fanned out across the country to conduct operations. The hierarchy within these structures was mostly shrouded in darkness and was a frequent topic of speculation. Even various high-ranking Afghan officials, including the president himself, were presumably not privy to many of their activities. That being said, one thing appears beyond dispute: control of the intelligence agency ultimately resided in Langley, Virginia, at the headquarters of the CIA, without whose approval and support the NDS would have ceased to function. Ahmad Zia Saraj, the NDS's last acting director, also had to be approved by US intelligence before being considered for the position. "That was only allowed with the CIA's okay. Otherwise, it would never have been possible," an Afghan security analyst told me on the condition of anonymity. The nature of this relationship was established in practice as soon as NATO troops invaded back in 2001. "Company men" such as Greg Vogle, a close associate of Hamid Karzai and former chief of the CIA's station in Kabul, insisted on expanding the agency's shadowy structures in Afghanistan in order to search for terrorists. To this end, recruits were solicited from two groups above all: former employees of the Northern Alliance and ex-KHAD officials, the Kabul-based intelligence agency built by the KGB in the 1980s.

To some, it might seem paradoxical that Washington would enter into this de facto alliance with former enemies, for during the Cold War, the KHAD had targeted the mujahideen rebels whom the United States and its allies supported. Most of the victims of this infamous intelligence agency were civilians, and its war crimes have still yet to be genuinely confronted. Similar to the case of Syrian intelligence officials who have fled to Europe in recent years, a number of KHAD war criminals can be found in Germany and the Netherlands today. After the fall of the Communist regime in Kabul, both countries became popular destinations among Afghans who had been members of the PDPA and served in the regime's military or intelligence apparatus.[112] While the KHAD's victims continue to process their trauma and search for the hastily buried remains of relatives it once kidnapped and murdered, several of the agency's former figureheads have made a comeback of sorts thanks to the War on Terror. War criminals such as Mohammad Najibullah, the last Communist dictator of Afghanistan and probably the most notorious KHAD director, are now celebrated as heroes, their terror regime relativized and romanticized. For its own part, the CIA relied on the one-time KGB apprentices, whom it viewed as suitable and well-trained intelligence agency material. In contrast, the recruits from the Northern Alliance milieu appeared less professional, which is why many were sent to the US to receive training. The most notorious example is Amrullah Saleh, Afghanistan's last serving vice president.

In the early years of the Karzai era, Saleh climbed the ladder to become the head of NDS. Since then, he has been accused of committing numerous war crimes by various human rights organizations. NDS prisons were among the most brutal outgrowths of the War on Terror. They were places where even the most unimaginable torture methods were used regularly. In Afghans such as Saleh, the Americans found just the people to do their dirty work. Saleh's predecessor, Muhammad Arif Sarwari, was similarly infamous. Sarwari, who immediately assumed the post of NDS director after the fall of the Taliban, was once a key figure in the intelligence agency of the mujahideen leader Ahmad Shah Massoud. Once the mujahideen captured Kabul in the 1990s, Sarwari took over the KHAD and began a collaboration with the Communist intelligence officials in Kabul. This same alliance was resurrected by the War on Terror. For example, one NDS director was the famous ex-Communist Masoom Stanekzai, who gained notoriety during the Ghani years for expanding the use of brutal raids that claimed numerous civilian lives. Although growing criticism eventually pressured Stanekzai to resign, he went on to lead the Afghan government's negotiation team during peace talks with the Taliban.

Over the course of the US occupation, the NDS developed into a mafia-like intelligence network with virtually unlimited resources at its disposal thanks to the CIA. Not only did the crimes of the KHAD go unaddressed, a KHAD 2.0 was created in the form of the NDS, which perfected the KGB's brutal interrogation methods with the help of the CIA. In spite of the clear hierarchy between the Americans and the Afghans, NDS agents managed time and again to take advantage of their positions. They pursued personal vendettas, unreservedly bombed civilians for ideological reasons, and used the millions of dollars from Washington and Langley to build up personal fiefdoms that they maintained through both terrorism and human and drug trafficking. One figure who particularly embodied this criminal lifestyle is Asadullah Khalid, Afghanistan's defense minister towards the end of the occupation. Khaled had previously served as director of the NDS and as governor of various provinces. Several international human rights organizations attest that in all of the positions he held, he committed grievous human rights abuses including torture, sexual abuse, and murder. According to reports, Khaled had personal torture dungeons at his residences in the provinces of Kandahar and Ghazni. He also had young girls kidnapped and held them as sex slaves. According to an in-depth exposé by CBC News, he also ordered the murder of five United Nations workers who had posed a risk to his lucrative drug business. Khaled's numerous wrongdoings were even discussed in Canada's parliament in 2009. Ultimately, the Canadian politicians more or less concluded that their country had allied with some highly problematic actors.[113]

It was obvious that figures such as these were not simply going to disappear overnight. The NDS and the paramilitary units of the CIA are among the bloodiest consequences of the War on Terror in Afghanistan. Though they no longer exist in the same form since the withdrawal of NATO troops and the Taliban's recapture of state power, their legacy persists in the General Directorate of Intelligence (GDI), the intelligence agency set up by the Taliban. And indeed, their brutality ultimately strengthened the Taliban, as can be seen in the example of Khost Province. For years, large swaths of Khost had been controlled by the so-called Khost Protection Force (KPF), a paramilitary organization founded by the CIA. Notorious for its numerous human rights violations, the KPF routinely kidnapped, tortured, and murdered civilians.[114] While conducting research in Khost back in 2017, I had my first personal encounter with the CIA militia. Deliberately not mentioning my work as a journalist, I said I was a visitor from Kabul. Otherwise I may have run into the same fate as the Afghan BBC journalist Ahmad Shah.

In April 2018, Shah was killed by "unknown gunmen," as several media outlets reported. Yet it was an open secret that the KPF had murdered the journalist after threatening him multiple times. Although local journalists were aware of the KPF's involvement in the case of Ahmad Shah, they would have endangered both themselves and their families had they reported this information. The militia mainly hunted those journalists and human rights activists who focused on the war crimes it and the Americans committed in the region. For this reason, several colleagues in Khost with whom I have worked in the past have explicitly requested I not publish their names.[115] The terror regime of the KPF fomented extremism in the region for years. Many victims of the militia have now joined the Taliban, making Khost a particularly apt illustration of the myopia of the American counterterrorism struggle. "As soon as their high pay dries up, they are going to pillage this city," a merchant from the province told me during my research.

Fifth Failure: Unleashing Refugee Waves

When I first stood outside of the passport office in Kabul eight years ago, it was as if all hell had broken loose. Hundreds or perhaps even thousands of people were standing around in the sweltering heat. Many of them had come from other provinces and arrived in the middle of the night to claim a place in line. The reason was simple: they wanted to get out of Afghanistan so that they could finally live in safety. They therefore needed to apply for a passport, which is not something most Afghans have. That same year, the old handwritten Afghan passports had been invalidated and replaced by a new biometric version that made it easier to check the identity of the owner. The timing of the new passport's introduction was no coincidence. That summer—the summer of 2015, to be precise—hundreds of thousands of Afghans set out towards Europe with other refugees from Syria, Somalia, and Iran. This occurrence is still referred to as the "refugee crisis" and remains a topic of heated debate in talk shows and op-ed pages. For its own part, the Afghan government sought to turn a profit off the refugee wave. A new passport cost 5,000 Afghani, or approximately $75. Many Afghans wanted to use their passports to flee to Pakistan, Iran, or Turkey, as the violence in the country was escalating. While Ghani's unstable power apparatus was busy "governing," a spate of suicide attacks and Taliban bombings had struck multiple urban centers in Afghanistan. Around the same time, the Afghan ISIS cell had come into existence, further escalating the conflict. At the root of the dilemma, however, was the War on Terror.

In 2015, the Afghanistan War was one of the deadliest conflicts in the world. Already back then, it was clear that the NATO intervention in the country—officially renamed in 2015 from Operation Enduring Freedom to Resolute Support Mission—was not going to achieve any of its goals. Afghanistan was becoming more rather than less dangerous. The majority of the population had felt zero effects of Western aid and grown poorer while corrupt political elites had been off jet-setting and spending most of their time abroad. Extremist groups had not been deprived of their breeding ground but instead further strengthened. The number of Taliban fighters was steadily increasing, while an entirely new actor was emerging in the form of ISIS. Meanwhile, the responsible parties had no desire to confront these realities. For Germany and other European states in particular, the real problem was the stream of refugees from Afghanistan. The politicians in charge knew that the "good war" and "nation building" had turned into a disaster. Yet they did not want to admit this to the public.

This kind of politics has had some bizarre consequences. Some of these can be seen at an institution in downtown Kabul named Hotel Spinzar, located near the lively main street, the old bazaar, and the famous Mosque of the King of Two Swords. Countless pedestrians walk by the hotel every day without ever taking notice. When I visited in early 2021, it looked just as inconspicuous as any of the other somewhat dilapidated buildings in the area. Though Spinzar translates to "white gold," the hotel lacks any signs of opulence. In fact, the reality there is fairly bleak. A bored-looking guard sits in front of the entrance, giving the occasional visitors only a fleeting once-over. The receptionist stares at the screen of his smartphone, ringing guests when requested. The lobby is empty aside from a few dusty pieces of furniture, as is the dining room. All things considered, Spinzar would be entirely unremarkable—if it did not receive several groups of rejected asylum seekers per week.

These people have been deported from any number of countries. While I was visiting, Afghans sent back from Germany, Austria, and Iran had recently been checked in by the authorities, the first step into their new old life. For about seven years, the hotel has been a partner of the International Organization for Migration (IOM). Many of its guests are desperate people with no place to go in Kabul. Once they have arrived at the Kabul airport, they are virtually forced to stay at the hotel—if they do not wish to sleep on the street. I spoke to two men who had arrived a couple of hours ago, Jawed Hussaini, age twenty-seven, and Taheb Shinwari, age twenty-eight. They had been living in Vienna only one day before. Now they were in Kabul, where the last several days alone they had seen several car bomb detonations and disturbances caused by criminal gangs. The Taliban controlled more than half of the country at the time, including regions only a few kilometers outside of the capital. Nevertheless, deportations continued apace. In 2016, approximately one year after the "great refugee summer" had broken out, the European Union signed a refugee deal with the government of the Afghan president, Ashraf Ghani. European countries such as Germany and Austria then began conducting group deportations of

Afghan refugees, shipping them back to the war-torn dystopia on charter flights or Turkish Airlines and Qatar Airways planes. This whole situation appeared even more paradoxical after I experienced one of these flights firsthand.

On any given flight from Istanbul to Kabul—a particularly popular route for deportations (and all manner of other trips) to Afghanistan—journalists, diplomats, NGO workers, and wealthy Afghan politicians would travel in the same plane with deported refugees. In one particularly bizarre scene, I recognized Maryam Solaimankhil, a famously corrupt member of parliament who grew up in California and holds US citizenship, sitting in first class on a plane that was filled only a few rows behind her with Afghans being sent back from Istanbul. Turkey is another state that participated in the mass deportation of Afghan refugees, while rich Afghans—typically members of the political elite—managed to buy their way into the country, easily obtaining Turkish citizenship by investing in real estate. When I saw her, Solaimankhil had her hands full with shopping bags from famous luxury brands. The refugees sitting behind her were probably hoping for a few dollars in aid money from the IOM in Kabul.

"I was told that I'd receive money upon arrival. I'm still waiting for it," Jawed Hussaini told me when I met him in Spinzar in 2021. After more than five years in Innsbruck, Austria, he submitted to his "voluntary return." It was not entirely voluntary, though that is how it was categorized in the statistics—as opposed to a forced deportation. While Hussaini was beset with family problems, he was denied all hope of a future in Austria. "There was nothing left for me to do but return. I felt increasingly unwell and became depressed. The authorities made me feel like I wasn't human," he told me. In Innsbruck, he sometimes worked charity gigs organized by the refugee shelter for which he received a token payment of a few Euros, though he never received a work permit. He'd stroll through the city in the evenings, sometimes treating himself to a beer in a bar called Moustache. When I heard that name while sitting in Spinzar, I looked up from my notes. Years ago, I'd worked at Moustache as a bouncer, and it's a place I still enjoy going regularly. Discovering this overlap I had with Hussaini gave me a strange feeling. While he will likely never again see the bar in Innsbruck's old town, I enjoy any manner of freedoms simply due to a piece of paper that he was denied. This thought refused to leave my head as I listened to him. Back in the summer of 2015, Hussaini had set out with numerous other refugees towards Europe. His journey began not in Afghanistan but Iran, the country of his birth and where his family still lives along with hundreds of thousands of other members of the Hazara ethnic group. During the civil war years of the 1990s, many Hazaras fled Afghanistan to Iran, the majority of whose population is also Shia. Ever since, the Hazaras—who are easily recognizable from their Asian facial features and their Hazaragi dialect—have been subjected to institutional and social racism in their neighboring country. Nevertheless, Hussaini still told me that he planned to return to Iran. "I don't know anyone in Kabul. The city is foreign to me," he explained. At the time we spoke, Hussaini's father was old and infirm. In Maidan Wardak near Kabul, the native Afghan province of Hussaini's family, war had been raging for years. Almost the entire province had come under control of the Taliban. Furthermore, there had been an increase in ethnic tensions between Hazara and Pashtun nomads. "I could be in Wardak in forty minutes, but that would be suicide. The situation in Kabul is bad enough," Hussaini said, telling me about how he hoped to start a family in Iran. He was finished with Europe.

Taheb Shinwari had different plans and a different refugee history. The bearded Pashtun hails from the eastern Nangarhar Province. One of Afghanistan's most troubled regions in recent years, Nangarhar bore witness to the Afghanistan War in all its horrid diversity—from ISIS, to the Taliban, to Afghan CIA militias that mostly killed civilians, to daily drone strikes. It was also where the so-called Mother of All Bombs—the US military's largest non-nuclear bomb—was dropped in April 2017 in what marked the high point of violence in the province. Shinwari left Afghanistan that same year. After a suicide attack targeted local security forces, he felt he had to flee. The reason for this was that he himself had been a member of a militia fighting the Taliban on behalf of the government. Shinwari is hardly exceptional in this regard. Afghanistan's younger generation has known virtually nothing but war and is deeply entangled with it. During the occupation, all sides recruited young men and often even minors. Shinwari had had enough of this life. After getting together several thousand dollars, he left Afghanistan. Only three years later did he make it to Austria, after spending time in Iran and several other countries along his escape route. Upon arriving in Vienna shortly after the start of the COVID pandemic in 2020, he met many other Afghans with similar stories to his own. To him, life in Austria's capital was different: it was comfortable and safe. Shinwari thought he had finally reached his destination. He could stroll through the streets with friends without worrying that a bomb might explode. There were no checkpoints, weapons, or violence.

"In Vienna, you can live and start a family. I dreamt of opening a grocery store or cell phone shop," he recalled during our conversation. However, his dream proved short-lived. The Austrian authorities decided that his story was implausible, that the reason he gave for fleeing may have been fabricated. Afghanistan had enough "safe" regions where one could live, they argued. Shinwari's asylum application was rejected. A lawyer had taken his case for free.

On February 19, 2021, Shinwari was picked up by the police and put in an airplane. He was furious, but he did not resist. "A lot of the people deciding our fate have no idea what's happening in Afghanistan. They would never dare to go there. But I have to," he told me. The people of whom he spoke include the Austrian and German court-appointed experts charged with assessing the security situation on the ground in Afghanistan. A famous example of one of these so-called experts is Karl Mahringer, an Afghanistan assessor from Austria who left his position in 2019 after coming under fire for the shoddiness of his work. For years, Mahringer had been a fixture before the court, responsible not only for Afghanistan but also Iraq and Syria. Most of his "analyses" read like travel diaries. Another famous assessor is the Afghan-Austrian political scientist Sarajuddin Rasuly. In 2021, he spoke in favor of deportations to Afghanistan, claiming that it was possible to lead a safe life in Kabul and the western city of Herat. The data and findings on which Rasuly based his claim remain unclear, as does the date of his last trip to Afghanistan.[116] The fact that people such as these were the ones deciding the fates of Afghan asylum seekers was a scandal for Hussaini and Shinwari.

Sitting in Spinzar, the two deportees were visibly tired and dejected. "Some years ago, a young man committed suicide in the hotel after being deported. Only then did people start to notice what is going on here," I was told by a bookseller whose stand was located near the hotel. The man of whom he spoke was named Jamal and had been deported from Germany in July 2018. He was one of "Seehofer's 69"—the sixty-nine Afghan refugees that the German minister of the interior, Horst Seehofer, famously bragged about deporting on his sixty-ninth birthday. Spinzar profits from its partnership with the IOM. Nevertheless, the hotel takes the deportees' problems seriously. "We don't support their deportation. They have taken tremendous risks to escape the war. The fact that they are brought back in the end, sometimes with violence, is painful for us as well," a receptionist by the name of Jawed Noori explained to me. In recent months and years, suicide attacks and other bombings had also occurred near Spinzar. This is not surprising, for it is not far from the Afghan foreign ministry and other institutions of the government and military that are regularly targeted by terrorist groups. A night in Spinzar including meals costs 1,000 Afghani, slightly more than $11. This is covered by the IOM, yet it is deducted from the total sum of money the deportees receive from the organization to get themselves on their feet after their return. So-called voluntary returners receive slightly more money than those deported completely against their will with the use of force. At most, however, a deportee never receives more than a few hundred dollars—hardly enough to get a person very far.

Abdul Ghafoor, a Hazara in his mid-thirties, knows perhaps more about deportations to Afghanistan than anyone else. After making it all the way to Norway, he was deported in 2013. Shortly thereafter, he founded Afghanistan Migrants Advice and Support Organization (AMASO), an NGO that advocates for the interests of deportees. Once a one-man operation, AMASO now employs four other Afghans. Its office is in the famous Kabul district of Pul-e Surkh, a place always bustling with activity. "Deportations to Afghanistan are a huge mistake. The security situation on the ground is often intentionally misconstrued to justify repatriations and deportations," Ghafoor explained to me in the spring of 2021. His NGO primarily attends to marginalized deportees with no connections to the country. He has met countless young men like Hussaini and Shinwari. Many of them are no longer reachable, having plunged themselves into a second attempt to escape. In view of the escalating security situation, the wave of refugees will not soon come to an end. "Most of them are probably somewhere in Iran," Ghafoor said. Meanwhile, he tries to help those who have stayed in Afghanistan. AMASO offers workshops and cheap rooms in shared apartments. It also raises money to help deportees get established and tries to find them jobs. Ghafoor's most important message to his clients is that deportation does not have to be the end of the world. He knows that this might sound too optimistic, which is why he continues to appeal to EU states to impose bans on deportations to Afghanistan. When I spoke to Taheb Shinwari, he had resigned himself to a future in Afghanistan, ultimately concluding he would not be able to escape the life he had once left behind. "I have to go back to Nangarhar. I'll be recruited by the militia again there. There's no other work there, and in Kabul I have nothing and no one," he summed up. Shinwari's district of Nangarhar had already been recaptured by the Taliban at the time of our conversation.

Mohammadi once fought for the Afghan army with his brother, but he decided to flee after the latter was killed. He managed to make it to Germany and start afresh. However, his new life was abruptly ended in July 2018. "They deported me because that guy [Seehofer] had a birthday. Isn't that unbelievable?" a dumbfounded Mohammadi asked when I met him in Kabul in early 2021. Since

2016, Germany had deported more than a thousand Afghans. Supposedly, the deportees have been mainly single men with criminal histories, yet human rights organizations have repeatedly pointed out that young families have also been separated and that not all deportees have had rap sheets. In March 2020, Germany suspended deportation flights upon the request of Afghan authorities due to the COVID pandemic. They resumed again in December of that year. For Mohammadi, developments such as these are an unprecedented scandal. "In Afghanistan, there are no human rights to speak of. But Europe isn't really better in this area. Most of the deportees are not criminals. They've been busted for things like riding public transit without a ticket, which is also counted as a criminal offense," he said.

When we spoke, Mohammadi had since gotten married and become a father. He was also preparing for his pending return to Germany. Thanks to the friends and lawyers who championed his case, he was not only granted a visa to re-enter the country but also allowed to bring his young family with him. "I love Afghanistan, but I've had enough of my country. Death is too omnipresent here. I have to think of my family," he told me. July 2021 saw the fortieth German deportation flight since the Joint Way Forward agreement between the EU and the Afghan government. The last German troops had withdrawn from Afghanistan several days before. Amid the war and the pandemic, the German government was continuing to deport Afghan refugees, as were the governments of many other countries. Although various human rights experts criticized this practice, it appeared to have been normalized by politics. In Berlin, Vienna, and elsewhere, authorities continued to claim that there were safe regions in Afghanistan. Yet the corrupt Afghan government is also to blame. "Our politicians have sold us out," Khayesta Mohammadi told me furiously when the topic came up. Indeed, the Afghanistan government only signed the deportation agreement so that it could continue to receive aid money from the EU. Meanwhile, at the time when the agreement was made, leading Afghan politicians and their families had long left the country themselves. The children of President Ashraf Ghani, who was once a refugee himself, have lived in the United States for decades, the country of their birth. Nevertheless, Ghani has always found harsh words for the wave of Afghan refugees, something that has hurt his popularity. In a March 2016 interview with the BBC, the Afghan president stated that he had "no sympathy" for Afghan refugees, whom he accused of "break[ing] the social contract" with their departure.[117] Shortly after the withdrawal of NATO troops was announced for 2021, Ghani claimed that his government was prepared for the Taliban. "Whoever is afraid should leave," he said in one of his speeches. In the following weeks, dozens of districts in the north of the country were taken over by the Taliban, while Afghan soldiers surrendered without a fight or fled. Kabul then requested a suspension of deportations, though various European countries continued deporting anyway. Those in power were apparently unconcerned by the fact that a deportation sometimes amounts to an indirect death sentence. This was underscored in July 2021, when it came out that a deported Afghan in Baghlan Province—one of the country's most troubled regions for years—had been killed in a grenade attack. In view of the mass deportations and the high death count from the war, any assumption that this was an isolated incident appears more than implausible.

Sixth Failure: The Fairy Tale of Women's Liberation

"I'm afraid that Afghan women and girls are going to suffer unspeakable harm," George W. Bush told the German broadcaster *Deutsche Welle* in July 2021. "They're just going to be left behind to be slaughtered by these very brutal people, and it breaks my heart."[118] Of all people, Bush was alarmed by NATO's withdrawal from Afghanistan—and he sought once again to convince the public that his "crusade" had improved the position of Afghan women. His factually untrue statements went unchallenged by *Deutsche Welle*, which effectively gave the war criminal a PR platform.

The liberation of Afghan women has long been among the key arguments for military intervention in the Hindu Kush. In fact, this argument predates the American War on Terror, going all the way back to both the colonization attempts of the British crown and the invasion of the Soviet troops. As the last lines of the first edition of this book were being written back in 2021, talk of the "betrayal" or "abandonment" of Afghan women was ubiquitous in the media. This discourse implies that only the West is capable of saving Afghan women from their "savage" fathers, husbands, brothers, and sons. Meanwhile, it disguises the fact that Western powers have never invaded Afghanistan for the sake of women. They have simply been concerned with their own interests. This is evident from the alliances the West formed with brutal warlords and human rights abusers who were every bit as regressive as the Taliban and other extremists when it came to women's rights. These actors, who included famous politicians, warlords, and religious clerics, often mocked and disparaged ambitious women who dared to question their positions, even insulting them on live TV. Their targets were often female journalists, activists, and politicians. A prominent example is Malalai Joya, the former member of parliament turned women's and human rights activist. During a parliamentary session in 2005, Joya criticized several of her male colleagues, accurately pointing out that they and many other "democratically elected" politicians in Kabul were in fact war criminals who only few years prior had reduced the country to rubble. Joya was then cursed, attacked both verbally and physically, and expelled from the chamber, even though she had merely brought up a reality that the West suppresses to this day: the ostensible liberators never cared about women's rights in Afghanistan. They were solely concerned with their own power and the War on Terror, which only added to the suffering of millions of Afghan women and girls. This is particularly obvious in those places in Afghanistan that are rarely visited by Western journalists.

One such place is Badikhel, a village near the Pakistan border in Khost Province. Around 250 families live here, including the family of Habib ur-Rahman, a broad-shouldered man in his early fifties. A former pilot in the Afghan military, ur-Rahman was forced into retirement by heart problems. Shortly thereafter, he moved with his family back to his native village, where he began operating a small girls' school—on a volunteer basis and out of his own house. During the days, he teaches about thirty students in his living room, and in the evenings, he pushes the desks and chairs aside and spreads out mattresses for himself and his family to sleep on. Although the Taliban had not yet taken over when he founded the school, the extremists' influence had risen sharply in the region, just as it had in many other parts of Afghanistan. This made Habib ur-Rahman's educational project all the more revolutionary. When they were in power during the 1990s, the Taliban closed numerous girls' schools, denying millions of Afghan girls an education and a chance to work. Now, however, even some active Taliban members from the region send their daughters, sisters, and nieces to ur-Rahman's home school. More generally, the extremists are not the only problem the teacher has encountered. He has also had to win over many skeptical fellow villagers. Afghanistan's rural regions are home to some extremely conservative social structures that cannot simply be torn down—especially not with violence. They can, however, be changed for the better by local grassroots movements that adopt a constructive and sustainable approach. Habib ur-Rahman's initiative is the best example of this. Over time, he has managed to convince numerous families to send their daughters to his school. Every morning until the noon prayer, they study math, geography, Islamic religion, history, and their native Pashto.

During the first Taliban regime, a girl's school in Badikhel—not to mention one run by a man—would have been unfathomable. Yet the villages have also changed since that time. Habib ur-Rahman claims that many of the extremists from his village have no problem with his school. "Their female relatives attend my school while they themselves fight and hide. The Taliban fighters don't live in our village anymore, but they've encouraged the girls to attend school. Their girls' education is important to them," he told me back in 2021. When the Taliban took power in the 1990s, they put their patriarchal extremist values into practice. Women were de facto banned from walking on the street without a close male relative, and girls' schools were banned in many parts of the country. Before taking power again in 2021, the Taliban leadership's statements about the issue were deliberately vague. "We do not want to ban education and work for women. However, we have certain Islamic norms that are important to us. We don't live in the West," Sher Mohammad Abbas Stanekzai emphasized in several interviews back 2020 while serving as a member of the Taliban delegation in Qatar. A senior Taliban official, Stanekzai went on to become Afghanistan's foreign minister when the Taliban came back to power in September 2021. How exactly these norms were to be observed was a question that even the extremists often could not answer at the time. Meanwhile, many Afghans justifiably pointed out the hypocrisy of the Taliban leaders during their Qatari exile, where they lived with their entire families and sent their sons and daughters to expensive private schools far more liberal than Afghan educational institutions. For its own part, the girls' school in the village of Badikhel is hardly a modern elite university. Yet it illustrates how paradoxical and complex the situation on the ground in Afghanistan can be. While some Taliban fighters send their female relatives to ur-Rahman's school, others have sent him threats. "These threats target not only the core of my work but me and my family personally. This of course doesn't make life here any easier," he said.

The Taliban's contradictory behavior in Badikhel comes as no surprise to experts on the region. According to the political ethnographer Orzala Nemat, the director of the Kabul-based Afghanistan Research and Evaluation Unit (AREU), the extremists already acted similarly in the late 1990s: "The Taliban were never able to convince their own men of their basically deeply un-Islamic diktats, such as the closing of girls' schools," she says. Like many other Afghans, Nemat is of the opinion that the Taliban act in a way that is fundamentally opposed to Islam and are ignorant of their religion. After all, the oldest continuously operating institution of higher learning in the world, the University of al-Qarawiyyin in the Moroccan city of Fez, was founded by the Muslim philanthropist Fatima al-Fihri as far back as the ninth century. The city of Khost is now home to a university as well. When we spoke, Habib ur-Rahman's sons were studying there. "One of them will be a doctor, the other an engineer. They make me quite proud," he said. For their father's school, the two sometimes procure textbooks in the city or fill in as substitute teachers. The university is also the goal of ur-Rahman's own students. "I want to attend uni one day. I want to be a doctor or teacher and serve my people," I was told by Latifa, the sister of a Taliban fighter. This would have required her to attend secondary school in the city, as Habib ur-Rahman's home school only goes through sixth grade. However, the Taliban have now banned girls and women from attending secondary school and university, leaving Latifa's dreams in doubt.

Ur-Rahman receives virtually no support. The few writing implements in his classroom have been purchased with donations from the villagers. In Afghan villages, the lack of educational offerings owes not only to the Taliban and their ideology. "I wonder whether the government even knows if I'm running a school in my own house. A lot of people talk about schools and universities in the capital, but what about the villages?" he asked. During the two decades of occupation, the US government alone pumped around a billion dollars into the Afghan educational system. The goal was to create hundreds of new schools and fill classrooms with female students. Instead, much of this money ended up in the pockets of corrupt warlords and politicians. Funding was acquired for schools, while the schools themselves sat empty. An exposé by the American journalist Azmat Khan revealed that in 2015, at least 1,100 schools were being operated by the Afghan ministry of education, though instruction was actually taking place in only a fraction of them. Referred to by critics as "ghost schools," they existed only on paper. In reality, they were a tool for laundering money.[119] Many of them were even specifically designated as girls' schools in order to promote the flow of Western money.

"Our school is real, but no one seems to care. Western aid money has never reached this corner of Afghanistan," ur-Rahman said. He knows that this will not change any time soon. People in

Khost make a living primarily from their own hard work. While both men and women in the province work in the fields and devote their summers to the harvest, many men from Khost travel to the United Arab Emirates as labor migrants, where they drive taxis or work in construction or the restaurant industry. They reinvest their earnings in Khost, which has now grown into a sizeable city. These economic structures are one reason why many of its residents have not joined the Taliban.

Nevertheless, once the United States had signed a withdrawal deal with the Taliban in early 2020, it was only a matter of time before the extremists returned to state power. In Afghanistan's urban centers, many already began to fear a return to the dark old days of the Taliban along with renewed educational bans for women and girls, although Ashraf Ghani's government in Kabul and the American negotiators claimed that they would not tolerate a return to such practices. "Going to school has always been difficult for Afghan women. But now I'm optimistic that things are slowly changing," I was told by Mahbuba, one of Habib ur-Rahman's students. At first, some of her family members had been against her attending school. By the time we spoke, however, all had come around: "They're even encouraging other relatives to send their daughters to school. Sending girls to school should be a matter of course, as we're an important part of Afghan society."

Positive achievements like the one in Badikhel have been brought about by Afghans themselves—without Western aid. Nevertheless, many Western observers continue to believe that Afghan women can only be "liberated" by an external invasion, even though the two decades of occupation produced deeply misogynistic structures. Corrupt and hungry for power to boot, such structures stand in the way of progressive projects such as Habib ur-Rahman's. The Kabul government and its Western allies may claim to champion the rights of women, but they usually tread on these rights. In the capital city alone, thousands of women now beg for money or work as prostitutes while supposed women's rights activists become rich by promoting themselves to the West.

One example is the politician and former presidential candidate Fawzia Koofi. She was also part of the very delegation that represented the Afghan occupation government in its negotiations with the Taliban. Within Afghanistan, Koofi is above all known for her corruption and dubious business dealings. In 2015, the Revolutionary Association of the Women of Afghanistan (RAWA), one of the most famous women's rights organizations in the country, published an article describing Koofi's "true colors." Among other things, it accused her of connections to drug kingpins and warlords. Thomas Ruttig, an Afghanistan expert from Germany, has also explicitly mentioned Koofi's name in his writings on the machinations of the country's corrupt political elite. According to reports by Ruttig and others, Koofi's brothers run a mafia-like smuggling network in their home province of Badakhshan and are involved in the drug trade. Afghan media outlets have reported sporadically on Koofi's family and their criminal entanglements. Since the peace talks with the Taliban, Koofi has been interviewed and profiled by numerous Western media outlets. Most of these articles have resolutely ignored the accusations against her, instead depicting her as an upstanding, heroic woman who defied the Taliban. Along these lines, she was even nominated for the Nobel Peace Prize in 2020.[120]

When it came to the issue of women's liberation in Afghanistan, some Western media outlets played a frequently disastrous role, even inventing entire stories to promote certain narratives and worldviews. A famous example of this came about in the summer of 2010, when a photograph of the eighteen-year-old Aisha Mohammadzai—whose face had recently been mutilated—was featured on the cover of *Time* magazine. The image bore the caption "What Happens if We Leave Afghanistan." According to *Time*, the young Afghan woman was forced into an arranged marriage with a Taliban fighter. Following an attempted escape, the family of the man took revenge by cutting off her ears and nose. The award-winning photo set off a media debate, with many asking whether it was ethical to show a mutilated face on a magazine cover. Additional questions were raised about whether the facts corresponded to their presentation in the story.

Was the mutilation really perpetrated by the same extremists whom the West had hunted down in 2001? Or was it "merely" an instance of the same brutal domestic violence that continued to exist after the NATO invasion, including in many areas that were controlled by the occupation government and not the Taliban?

The cover story in *Time* linked the mutilation directly to the Taliban and the deployment of Western troops. This is a stretch, considering the years of various reports that have underscored that violence against women in Afghanistan is most prevalent in major cities. This fact complicates the *Time* story, for in contrast to the regions controlled by the Taliban at the time of the article, which were predominantly rural, the cities were controlled by the Washington-installed government. Yet the narrative of the barbaric Taliban fighter who oppresses his wife was apparently more enticing than a brutal "domestic drama" with no political background and no plausible link to Western troop deployment. In fact, as the Afghan news agency Pajhwok later reported, the Taliban had had nothing to do with the case. Of course, in view of the atrocity committed against Aisha Mohammadzai, one might view this detail as beside the point. Yet this detail was the central element on which *Time* built its story—a narrative with a potentially huge influence on political decisions, given that it was propagated by what was at the time one of the leading news magazines in the Western world. In spite of its reputation, this magazine was determined to use Aisha to construct its own story—a story that conformed to stereotypes and particular promoted worldviews, especially that of the fairy tale of the West's liberation of women in the Hindu Kush.

As someone who has spent years covering Afghanistan from both inside and outside the country, I know that this is nothing unusual. Virtually all journalists working on the ground in Afghanistan have at one point or another encountered professional colleagues who frantically chase down certain stories at the expense of facts. Most of them are white and Western, and many are male. They are always accompanied by interpreters and fixers, and they view the world through a thick Orientalist lens. As soon as they return to their countries of origin, they are regarded as established "experts" who deserve to be taken seriously, given their "familiarity" with the cultures and traditions they have encountered. After all, some of them can even utter a few scraps of the local language.

Sobering Realities

Life at the Factory

BACK IN THE spring of 2019, a woman wearing a *chaderi*, the Afghan word for burqa, entered a doctor's office with a toddler. She was feeling nauseated. Sayed Shah Mehrzad greeted her in the traditional Afghan manner, his right hand over his heart, and led her to a treatment room separated from the rest of the practice by a curtain. Several men were sitting in the waiting room. Hajii Niazi, an old Pashtun with a turban, had just been examined. Holding a bag of medicine in his hands, he flashed a toothless farewell smile to the others and wished them a nice day. The practice of Dr. Sayed Shah, as most call him, is located in Baghlan Province in northern Afghanistan. One of the most turbulent parts of the country, Baghlan borders Kunduz Province, the site of the 2009 air attacks ordered by the German colonel Georg Klein that claimed over 150 civilian lives. Following the attacks, it was alleged that the victims had been Taliban fighters. Just as is still the case, the war was rendered in black and white, with NATO and the Kabul government as the good guys and the Taliban as the bad. Yet Mehrzad knows as well as anyone that such constructs have little basis in reality.

During the Afghanistan War, which was often literally a war among brothers, the physician stood between the fronts, treating both Taliban fighters and soldiers in the Afghan army. "Often, there were situations where Talib and soldier lay injured side by side, wanting to go at each other," Mehrzad told me, his trademark flat cap in his hand as he wiped the sweat from his brow. When we spoke, Mehrzad wore a full brown beard and looked younger than his forty-six years of age. Among friends, he is known as a jovial character who likes to chat with everyone. Though Mehrzad grew up in Baghlan, his family originally hails from Kabul, and following the collapse of the Taliban at the end of 2001, he decided to make a new life for himself in the capital as a young doctor. This was during the first years of the presidential administration of Hamid Karzai, a time of palpable optimism particularly in Afghanistan's urban centers, and Mehrzad had been swept up in the mood as well. However, he would soon be disappointed. "In Kabul, you needed substantially more initial capital to open a practice with a pharmacy," he explained. To realize his dream back in 2005, he would have needed around $20,000. "I simply couldn't afford it, and nothing about that has changed since," he recalled. Mehrzad's wife and children still live in the capital, and he visits them regularly. "I love Baghlan, but I can't put all this on my family. Things are different in Kabul. Here, there's real war. And besides, there aren't any good schools or universities for my children," he said. Yet Mehrzad prefers Baghlan over Afghanistan's capital for a simple reason: the people in the province live as if they are part of one big family. They care about and help each other—in spite of, or perhaps because of, the war—and their relationships with each other often go back decades, the physician told me. The anonymity of Kabul isn't for him.

Traveling from Kabul to Baghlan by car requires driving for about four hours through the Salang Pass. It is one of the most beautiful routes in all of Afghanistan. Leading northward from Kabul, it runs through green valleys with crystal clear water. This region is also the location of the Panjshir Valley, the home of the famous mujahideen commander Ahmad Shah Massoud. In the spring of 2019, almost the entire stretch of highway leading north was plastered with pictures and billboards of Massoud and other fighters of his militia who had been killed. *Shaheed*, or "martyr," had been written everywhere. This word is now omnipresent in Afghanistan, which is hardly surprising, for there are many martyrs in the country—too many. Yet while the impoverished but relatively safe Panjshir become a kind of getaway destination for some of Kabul's residents during the war, hardly anyone made it up to Baghlan. The province mainly came to be known as a dangerous transit route for people heading to Mazar-e Sharif, the capital of Balkh Province and the location of the German Bundeswehr's headquarters. Anyone who could afford the plane ticket would fly to Mazar, though this category certainly didn't include the majority of Afghans. Meanwhile, the only people who traveled to Baghlan were those who had to, such as Mehrzad. In spite of all his love for the province, he is forced to stay by economic factors. "I've built everything here. I send most of the money to my family in Kabul. Without my income, they wouldn't be able to live," he said.

Baghlan is divided into several districts and regions. The provincial capital of Pul-e Khumri is home to a large bazaar with all the buzz of an Afghan city. There are fruit stands with famously juicy apples from the nearby district of Andarab, bananas stored in so-called banana houses, raisins, almonds, and tea. Young schoolgirls buy notebooks and pens while their mothers search for the choicest cuts of meat to prepare for dinner. Some women at the market wear *chaderi* whereas others don headscarves, sometimes loose and open. A few police officers patrol as children run around selling plastic bags to customers. The smells of fresh bread and raw meat intermingle with those of smoke and exhaust. Most of the buses and taxis coming from Afghanistan's capital stop here before picking up passengers to take them back to the capital. To get to Dr. Mehrzad's practice from Kabul, however, one needs to drive twenty minutes past Pul-e Khumri.

The physician works in an area referred to by the locals as the Factory. In the 1940s, a sugar factory was erected in this area with the aid of German engineers. This helped turn Baghlan into an industrial center and employment hub for people from the region. For northern Afghanistan, impoverished and abandoned by the country's power elite, this was a major step towards modernization. Entire families moved to Baghlan because of the factory, which remains intact today. The area prospered until war broke out in the late 1970s. In its bitter fight against the mujahideen, the Soviet puppet government in Kabul indiscriminately targeted the civilian population. Whether neighbors, friends, or relatives, anyone was liable to be suspected by the government of sympathizing with the rebels, or even of being a spy, murderer, or torturer. The war had driven a wedge through society, and many families had both mujahideen fighters and supporters of the Communist government. While the former believed in Allah and jihad, the latter held fast to Marx, Lenin, and the revolution.

One day after treating the old Pashtun and the woman in the *chaderi*, Dr. Mehrzad took in the early summer weather on the bank of the Kunduz River. Flowing through Baghlan, the Kunduz River is renowned for its superb pike, which are often served for breakfast in the province along with tea and bread. Mehrzad's practice is only a few minutes away from this tranquil place with hardly a soul far and wide. After some time, the peaceful atmosphere was disturbed by the rattling of an approaching motorcycle. A vehicle came into view carrying Mehrzad's driver. A young man with long hair, a beard, and a Kalashnikov dismounted and greeted the physician warmly. Twenty-three years old at the time, Lemar was a Taliban fighter, a fact he did nothing to hide. "We're on the right track, and God willing, we will win," Lemar said shortly after his arrival. By "we," he meant the Taliban, or the "Islamic Emirate of Afghanistan," as the movement calls itself. In front of him sat a plate of rice and meat. Like everyone else present, the Taliban fighter ate with his hands, and he consumed his food with gusto. Abdul Ghani, a resident of Baghlan and friend of Mehrzad, refilled his water glass and offered him vegetables and fruit. Mehrzad sat on the other side of the *disterkhan*, the tablecloth that is spread out on the floor at mealtimes in Afghanistan, busying himself with a toothpick. Lamb has a tendency to get stuck between teeth. As Lemar went on about the "holy war," incredulous over the fact that soldiers in the Afghan army are fighting the Taliban, Mehrzad seemed lost in thought. Though he did not share the views of the young fighter, whom he regards as completely naïve, he did not contradict him. The physician knew that the situation in Afghanistan during those final years of the occupation was too complicated for simple answers. Some young men enlisted in the army, and others joined the Taliban.

The complexity of the reality on the ground during those years is exemplified by the story of Abdul Ghani. When I spoke to him in 2019, the young father lived in what was at the time a "contested area"—what the Americans and their allies called those locations that went back and forth between being controlled by government troops and the Taliban. Ghani practically lived between the fronts, yet in his daily life, he mainly interacted with Lemar and other Taliban fighters, providing them with tea, fruit, and the odd meal. This was not what the haggard Ghani had imagined for himself. He had once wanted to build a new life for himself far away from the war in Baghlan. Yet in Kabul, he encountered the hostility with which many urban Afghans treat their compatriots from more rural regions—a hostility that is mostly a product of intra-Afghan racism and mistrust towards outsiders. "No one wanted to rent an apartment to me and my family. I was spit at and chased away because I'm a Pashtun. I was accused of having connections to the Taliban and called a terrorist," Ghani recounted indignantly.

After moving back to Baghlan, Ghani was forced into the very position he occupied when we spoke. Taliban fighters such as Lemar, whom Ghani had known since childhood, took advantage of their connections to him, endangering his family in the process. Ghani worried his house would be targeted by night raids or air strikes, even though he had no desire to associate with the Taliban. Yet he found himself in a complicated web of traditions and social norms from which he couldn't disentangle himself. These norms dictated that Ghani not deny hospitality to others, including Lemar and his companions. Ghani also felt contempt towards those Afghans who had forced him out of the capital. Afghanistan is a multiethnic country, and many of its regions are home to a number of communities that differ from each other considerably. Often, these communities peacefully coexist, as is usually the case in Baghlan. To this day, the Factory is home to Pashtuns, Tajiks, Hazaras, and Uzbeks, to Sunni and Shia Muslims. However, the increasingly ethnic nature of conflict in Afghanistan, particularly since the civil war years and the beginning of the War on Terror, means that tensions sometimes arise here as well. While political elites typically instrumentalize these tensions for their own interests and are quick to reconcile after feigned enmities, the situation is different among the general population. Mistrust, hostility, and contempt often linger. Ethnic trench warfare is often waged on the backs of ordinary people—ultimately affecting individuals such as Abdul Ghani, who is constantly linked to the Taliban because of his Pashtun background and his conservative and traditional outward appearance. He is hardly the only person to whom this happens. I myself have often been treated similarly in Afghanistan.

After we had eaten, tea was served. Sipping from his glass, Lemar turned his gaze towards Mehrzad. "The doctor is a friend of ours. He helps us and provides for us. We—the Emirate—value this greatly," he said. Mehrzad said nothing and looked slightly embarrassed. The young Talib was convinced that he was fighting evil, godless people. In the vast majority of cases, however, his enemies on the battlefield were neither foreign-born nor non-Muslim—read, occupiers—but rather his Afghan compatriots. One of Lemar's older brothers was a government employee. He worked for the governor of Baghlan, as Mehrzad would tell me later. Lemar's family had tried repeatedly to convince him to come home, but their efforts were in vain. Sayed Shah Mehrzad sees Lemar not first and foremost as a Taliban fighter but as the same young boy from his childhood. And in any case, Lemar is a patient of his, he said, as are several other Taliban fighters. "They're all just young guys desperately trying to romanticize this war. They grow out their hair and stop shaving, even though some of them are so young that they can hardly grow a beard. Of course, I help them when they're sick or injured and in need of treatment. That's my job. I don't have a choice," Mehrzad told me later, as he showed me pictures on his smartphone of other fighters who were Lemar's age. All of them sported long hair and beards, some of which were noticeably youthful. It was easy to get the impression that they viewed the war as an exciting Facebook drama, a chance to prove their masculinity. Some of the men in the photos had already fallen in battle. Mehrzad's oldest son, Elias, was living in Kabul at the time and studying medicine. He was also in his early twenties. Sometimes the doctor wonders whether his son too would have radicalized and joined the Taliban if he'd grown up in Baghlan. It's not hard to imagine, for in hardly any other area were so many young people being driven towards extremism and radicalization during the occupation.

Doctors and other medical personnel in Afghanistan were under constant pressure in the war years. Often, they became targets simply because they treated all sides equally. This was frowned upon mainly by the Americans and their local "counterterrorism" helpers. At times, the Hippocratic oath could even mortally endanger health care workers. This happened in Kunduz in 2016, when a hospital operated by the organization Doctors Without Borders was bombed by the US military. More than forty people died in the attack, all of whom were either medical personnel or patients. This was a PR disaster for the Pentagon. Nearly all observers of the war, including the United Nations, referred to the incident as a war crime, for even before the fighting in the city began, Doctors Without Borders had shared the coordinates of the hospital with all of the war parties. Both the Afghan and US military later alleged that Taliban fighters had been at the clinic, which Doctors Without Borders vehemently denied. After modifying their statement on the bombing multiple times, the Americans ultimately placed the blame on their Afghan allies, claiming that they had ordered the strike.

Around the same time, it came out that the clinic had already been targeted by Afghan special forces units several months before, when the building had been searched and its staff threatened. Back then as well, the clinic was accused of treating Taliban fighters. "The entire premise of the accusation is faulty. Even if an Afghan doctor treats Taliban, that can't be labeled a crime. It's our duty to help people," Mehrzad told me while seeing patients back at his practice. In the weeks and months before we spoke, he had been warned multiple times to watch his back. Word had gotten around that he was treating Taliban fighters—and a rumor was now being spread that he was one himself. The stress caused by these threats had evidently taken their toll on the physician, whose normally relaxed and jovial nature had all but disappeared. He bit his lips and seemed vaguely distracted. "What do they want from me?" he muttered to himself while taking the blood pressure of an elderly man. Sensing the doctor's irritation, the man tried to calm him: "Don't worry. Everyone here knows and respects you. We all love you. Nothing will happen to you!"

Late in the fall of 2019, the cold set in across Baghlan. Though the daily turmoil raged on, all appeared to be in order in Dr. Mehrzad's practice. The medicines sat sorted on their shelves, and the counter with the glass case looked new. The furniture shined. Not a single speck could be found on the curtain leading into the treatment room. Everything seemed as clean as ever. The only noticeable difference from before was that a heavy door with a thick, sturdy lock had been installed at the entrance of the practice. At the end of September, around six months after my first visit, Sayed Shah Mehrzad's practice had been firebombed. He recorded the aftermath with his smartphone: burned furniture and medicine packages can be seen in the video. Unknown culprits had broken open the door and thrown several incendiary devices into the rooms. No one had been present, and there were no witnesses. Standing amid his destroyed livelihood full of rage and sadness, Mehrzad swore in that moment that he was done with Baghlan. He couldn't go on like this, and he didn't want to either. How could the natives of the Factory—the same people he had known and helped for years—do something like this to him? Of course, not all of them were the culprits, but some of them certainly were, he thought. Had it been the soldiers, who simultaneously respected and loathed him? Or the Taliban, whom he constantly helped in spite of the all the risks? The answer will probably never be discovered. "Unknown perpetrator" has become one of the most frequently used turns of phrase by the Afghan press. Mehrzad's shock later turned into apathy. For a long time, he had stood between the fronts, which was something he could live with. Yet when his own practice became part of the front, a target of an attack, it was too much to bear. His physician's sense of duty and financial dependence aside, he wanted out. He resolved that he would first go to his family in Kabul, and that then—in the best-case scenario—they would get out of Afghanistan. Maybe they'd go to Europe, just as many other Afghans had done. His future lay elsewhere, or so he thought.

By the time we spoke, about eight weeks had passed since the firebombing. Sitting in the guest room of an old engineer friend named Farzad Sattar, Mehrzad spoke about the ongoing violence in Baghlan. The short route between Pul-e Khumri and the Factory had become the site of regular attacks, with burned-out vehicles regularly turning up on the road. Soldiers were now patrolling the streets, and Taliban fighters had taken to sniping from behind trees. "They shoot whenever they feel like it. And who do they hit? Civilians, of course," said Ahmad Agha, another friend of the physician and a Baghlan native. In front of him and the others stood cups of shimmering green tea along with both dried and fresh fruit. Agha reached for some golden raisins and a piece of *halwa-ye maqzi*, a special confectionary made of sesame seeds that is quite popular in northern Afghanistan. Meanwhile, Mehrzad fiddled with a knife and a pomegranate, apparently lost in thought. Opening the fruit gingerly at one end, he proceeded to split it five times. He then grabbed a tablespoon and hit it against the unopened end, causing the pomegranate's red seeds to rain down onto the plate below. Nothing ever came of Mehrzad's escape plan. Instead, he stayed in Baghlan and rebuilt his practice with the assistance of friends, relatives, and patients. "They've all helped me. With everything," he said. "Of course they did. Dr. Sayed Shah is Facebook friends with everyone in Baghlan," Sattar said with a smile. Mehrzad would not have been able to swing the renovation with his savings alone.

It was the natives of Baghlan's Factory who took him by the hand and refused to let him go. To this day, no one knows who the arsonists were. Lemar and his Taliban companions still haven't been back to the practice since hearing about the attack. However, the doctor keeps up on all his patients, including the "undesirable" ones. "Their families come here regularly. So I still hear about how they're doing. Sometimes, I prescribe them medicine," he said. As we spoke, an Afghan television station aired a brief report from Achin District in the eastern Afghan province of Nangarhar. In April 2018, a "Mother of All Bombs," the US military's largest non-nuclear bomb, had been dropped on the province. No precise account of the victims has ever been made. A wide swath of the surrounding area was cordoned off by American and Afghan soldiers immediately following the blast, while official reports claimed that the only casualties were "ISIS terrorists." Yet in the fall of 2019, the television report playing in Mehrzad's office suggested that the bomb was having lingering health effects. For several months, Achin residents had been witnessing a rise in skin diseases among children and adolescents. This was anything but surprising to Mehrzad. "I know these skin diseases quite well. They're also prevalent in Baghlan. Our country has been contaminated by bombs," he said. A special ointment, the only remedy that offers a modicum of relief, is prescribed by Mehrzahl frequently. "It's all we have, anyway," he said.

When we spoke, Dr. Mehrzad knew that much was about to change in Baghlan and the rest of Afghanistan. He was skeptical of both the peace talks with the Taliban and the Kabul government, which he believed had been conducting itself every bit as brutally as the former in the war ravaging the country. Regardless, Mehrzad had decided to carry on, to keep showing up at his practice day after day. As we spoke, a new patient came through the door, a police officer friend of his. "Well, doctor? Where's my medicine?" he bellowed. Laughing, the doctor tossed him a package. "It's for his mother," he told me. Mehrzad was going to keep treating both sides in both his practice and a few kilometers away, should he ever need to make a house call for Lemar and his companions. That's what he's there for—whether people like it or not.

The Man Who Gave Bush the Finger

The Sheraton Hotel in Doha, the capital of the Gulf emirate of Qatar, is a five-star palace that has it all. The interior architecture of the luminescent skyscraper comes off as both classical and futuristic. The word "lobby" does not do justice to the great hall replete with various cafés and restaurants. The grounds of the hotel feature several tennis courts, a fitness center, and an extensive wellness area. Nearby lies the Corniche, Doha's famous beach promenade, which usually fills up in the evenings with hotel guests, Qatari families with children, and guest workers with a little downtime. Amid the tumult, it is also possible to spot a few Afghans looking somewhat out of place.

On one evening in April 2019, a man in his early sixties by the name of Abdul Kadir Mohmand sat at a pub in the Sheraton eating kebab, grilled skewer delicacies that in Qatar make even the mouths of the famously carnivorous Afghans water. "Once you're here, all you can think about is food. Who cares about politics? Look at the bellies of the Taliban who live here," Mohmand told me between bites, as a waiter brought him freshly squeezed orange juice. Next to Mohmand on the table lay a thick photo album, which he guarded like a hawk. Several other Afghans who had also made the trip to Qatar sat at the table and glanced at it curiously. Twenty minutes later, everyone had eaten their fill and the table was cleared. Once tea had been served, Mohmand opened the album and launched into his past with all the verve of an experienced storyteller. After the Afghan Communists violently took power in Kabul forty years ago, a young Mohmand fled to the United States. As war raged in his homeland and the Soviet Union invaded during Christmas of 1979, Mohmand was beginning a new life for himself in America. He found a job at a well-known US company and married an American woman. Yet Afghanistan wouldn't release him from its grasp.

Mohmand is from an influential Pashtun family. His forefathers once successfully fought off the British—and now, foreign soldiers had once again invaded his homeland. Mohmand was one of the lucky ones, for many of his friends hadn't made it out of the country. They were now languishing in Pakistani refugee camps or hiding from the Soviet occupiers and the brutal regime in Kabul. A number of them had joined the mujahideen rebels and would go on to make a name for themselves as brave fighters in the coming years. Mohmand decided not to turn his back on his country. While on vacation from work, he flew to Pakistan. He then secretly crossed over the Durand Line into Afghanistan, joining the fight at the front against the Red Army. His album contains numerous photos from the "era of jihad," as he calls it. Some of them show him wearing a short full beard and an Afghan pakol hat, looking confidently into the camera. The battles against the Red Army shaped him. To this day, he cannot stand Communists—especially when they are his compatriots. "I do not forgive these people," he said, as he recounted the day when he had to bury a dozen children in Logar Province who had been killed by a Soviet air strike. "As I buried these innocent creatures with my own two hands, I made a vow to myself," he said.

Yet Mohmand did not travel to Qatar alone. Other exiled Afghans living in the US, the UK, Germany, Pakistan, and Saudi Arabia were also staying at the Sheraton, having been invited by the Qatari government for the first intra-Afghan dialogue in the Gulf emirate. The previous months had seen negotiations only between the Trump administration and the section of the Taliban's political leadership that had been living in exile in Doha for several years. The extremists first raised their flag in Qatar back in 2013, when they opened their office in the country. Afghanistan's president, Hamid Karzai responded indignantly. While critics accused the Gulf emirate of harboring fanatical extremists, more optimistic observers speculated that the Taliban had finally turned their backs on Afghanistan's archenemy Pakistan and were now open to a realistic conflict resolution in line with the interests of all Afghans.

Resembling a small fortress, the Taliban office had been built by Wahidullah Halimi, who also goes by the name Wahidullah Wardak. Halimi is not only extremely close to the Taliban but more or less a de facto member. He lived in Germany for a number of years and earned his engineering degree in Hamburg, though he is hardly unknown in Qatar. His Qatari construction firm, Gharnata, has built virtually half of Doha, including numerous government buildings. For him, designing and building the Taliban office was surely more ideologically than financially rewarding; perhaps he even did it as a personal favor. Interestingly, the office does not appear in Gharnata's online portfolio.[121]

The impending round of discussions was to be the first ever meeting between exiled Afghans, Taliban, representatives of Ashraf Ghani's government in Kabul, and members of Afghan civil society. Supposedly, the latter were being flown in on a chartered flight, but there had been no sign of them so far. In the meantime, Mohmand and the other guests discussed in the lobby and visited Doha, a desert city boasting impressive skyscrapers built by Bangladeshi and Pakistani guest workers alongside stables with expensive racehorses and marquee hunting falcons. Men and women walk the streets, almost all of them upholding Islamic conventions of dress. "I think the Taliban have been inspired by Qatar and want to create a similarly modeled state in Afghanistan," I was told by Daud Azami, an Afghan from Germany. A native of Frankfurt, Azami has been active in civil society for years. For him, it is important to underscore that both inside and outside Afghanistan there is a "third force," read, a strong civil society with no affinity for the Americans or the Afghan government. Meanwhile, Mohmand claimed that the situation in Afghanistan was mainly the fault of the Americans and the corrupt government in Kabul. To him, they were the ones who had spent the last twenty years destroying and plundering the country and acting like colonial occupiers, just as the Soviets and the British had done before them.

Mohmand has had to take a lot of flak throughout his life for his stance on the War on Terror. He was among the few US Afghans to oppose the Afghanistan War from the beginning, at a time when many of his compatriots became advisors to Bush and Cheney overnight and secured lucrative contracts. When Mohmand heard that Bush was making a campaign stop in his home state of Michigan back in 2004, the Afghan rewrote the sign outside of his restaurant to read, "Dogs allowed, Bush forbidden." When Bush got out of his tour bus and noticed the sign, he was indignant towards Mohmand, who responded in kind with his middle finger. "I am a grandson of Wazir Akbar Khan, who chased the British from Afghanistan. We will not kneel before you. Get lost!" he told the president.[122] This moment marked a turning point for Mohmand's family. Shortly after his confrontation with Bush, he received a citation for allegedly trying to attack the president. However, the Democratic attorney general of Michigan at the time took Mohmand's side against Bush's version of events, citing security camera footage that showed only a verbal confrontation. Yet Mohmand and his family were punished anyway. All of their business dealings were aggressively scrutinized by tax auditors. "We've been harassed ever since. It was obvious that this had to do with our anti-war position. Back then, Bush told the world that you were either with him or against him. This applied not only to states but to individuals like my father," I was told by Saidal Mohmand, the son of Abdul Kadir Mohmand.[123]

Yet Mohmand had once been a prominent representative of the Afghan diaspora in the United States. In the 1980s, he had helped arrange for several Afghans who had been injured fighting the Soviets to be flown to Michigan for medical treatment. He had maintained close contact with multiple senators and congressional representatives. One of them was Charlie Wilson, later played by Tom Hanks in the 2007 film *Charlie Wilson's War*. To this day, many believe that Wilson began pushing for Stinger missiles to be sent to the mujahideen rebels after learning about the suffering of the Afghan population by visiting a Pakistani refugee camp. Behind the scenes, however, Mohmand played an important role. Whereas many observers of the conflict continue to criticize the Reagan administration's decision to arm the rebels, Mohmand claimed, based on his own personal experience with air strikes by Soviet Mi-24 helicopters, that the rocket launchers would have saved the lives of numerous Afghans. The US government's relationship with him only changed after 2001, when he refused to support Washington's war in his native country.

At the Hotel with the Taliban

The purpose of the meeting in Doha was to discuss the events that unfolded at the end of 2001. It was seen as important that Afghans themselves confront what had happened together. The underlying assumption was that all of the participants involved bore responsibility for the worst atrocities of the past years, especially the Qatar-based Taliban delegation, who now found themselves faced with a number of important questions.

All of a sudden, Sultan Barakat appeared. A political science professor of Palestinian heritage and the director of the Doha Institute for Graduate Studies, Barakat had been the driving organizational force behind the Afghan meeting in Qatar. Now, he announced to those present that the intra-Afghan dialogue was being canceled. President Ashraf Ghani had not permitted the Kabul delegation to travel. The flights that had been chartered from Qatar Airways would have to return empty. Hundreds of thousands of Euros, mere peanuts to the Qatari government, had been spent for nothing. Bakarat wished the guests who had made it a pleasant stay—on the house—during their remaining days in Qatar. He also invited them to pay his institute a visit. Barakat has gray strands in his hair and speaks perfect English in a British accent due to his many years teaching in the UK. For decades, his focus has been peace and conflict studies. He believes—indeed justifiably—that the problems of the Middle East, North Africa, and Asia cannot be solved with the same Western theories that have created them. His institute, a state institution with particularly close ties to the foreign ministry of the Gulf emirate, is supposed to serve as a modern madrasa, as a repository of knowledge where solutions can be developed far beyond the confines of Eurocentrism. The university grounds make a sterile and futuristic impression. Modern and classical architecture intermingle here as well, but the campus seems empty, almost abandoned. "Whoever is familiar with universities in Europe or the US might think it seems boring here. Yet we're young and we hope to attract more students in the coming years," Barakat told our group as we visited the institute. When the issue of Qatar's ulterior motives in pushing for peace in Afghanistan came up, he struck a less idealistic tone. "Of course, geopolitical interests are at stake here. There's no point in denying it," he said.

For years, the Gulf emirate has been one of the world's largest producers of natural gas. In order to guarantee continued exports and prosperity for its population, the Qatari government seeks to tamp down on, if not eliminate, all conflict in the region. Along these lines, the war in Afghanistan is one of the largest obstacles to the geopolitical interests of Qatar, which relates to various other states in a similar manner. The region of contemporary Afghanistan has been traversed by some of the most important trade routes for centuries. This is one of the reasons why it has been the site of so many different conflicts for so long. In fact, during the NATO occupation, Afghanistan was afflicted by several proxy wars that generally went ignored in analyses of daily events. For example, whereas the Taliban were supported by Pakistan, the Afghan government maintained a close relationship to Islamabad's archenemy India. Moreover, a Sunni-Shia conflict became visible, exacerbated by the competition for regional influence between Saudi Arabia and Iran.

Another actor whose influence became increasingly obvious over the course of the war was the NATO member state Turkey. Turkey had wanted to take control of the international airport in Kabul following the planned withdrawal of Western troops, though these ambitions were thwarted when the Taliban swiftly recaptured the entire country in September 2021. Back in July, Turkish president Recep Tayyip Erdoğan had called upon the Taliban to "end the occupation of their brothers' soil." For years, the Erdoğan regime has maintained close contact with the warlord Abdul Rashid Dostum, a member of Afghanistan's Uzbek minority. In spite of concrete evidence that he has committed human rights abuses and torture, Dostum was given asylum in Turkey multiple times while the government in Ankara was deporting thousands of Afghan refugees. Though Turkey oppresses its own minority groups such as the Kurds, it likes to posture as a kind of defender of the Turkic peoples in Central Asia. In northern Afghanistan, the home of the Uzbeks and other ethnic groups that speak Turkic languages, Turkey sought to massively expand its influence towards the end of the occupation. In the summer of 2021, some observers even began reporting that Turkish killer drones were being deployed in Afghanistan. Finally, the rivalries of China and Russia with the Western world—read, NATO—also made their presence felt in Afghanistan.

Before the Taliban's ultimate seizure of power, a number of observers feared that the power vacuum created by NATO's planned withdrawal would be not only filled by problematic actors within Afghanistan but exploited by those states in the region that have long used the country as a geopolitical pawn, waging their wars on the backs of the Afghans. By all appearances, Qatar wants to put an end to this once and for all and hold Afghanistan's leaders accountable. Yet the Gulf emirate's role in this regard does not sit well with the Kabul government, which is why Ghani decided to pull the plug on the conference at the last minute. When the cancellation announcement was made, the only parties that had shown up were some exiled Afghans and the Taliban delegation, which Barakat and his employees had been "briefing" for several years. "They still have a long way to go," Barakat told me as he sat behind the wheel of his red sports car. Complaining about the obstinacy of the men in the black turbans, he stressed that they still had no clue how to act on the world stage.

The following day, some of the men in question appeared at the Sheraton, greeting the exiled Afghans with hugs and gestures of respect. "A bus is ready for you," a young man announced. He was wearing a full beard and *peran tonban*, the traditional Afghan combination of harem pants and a long shirt. Mohmand and the other guests started to advance. It was now obvious that the Taliban leadership in Qatar wanted to receive them. The bus's destination was another luxury hotel in Doha, though this one couldn't hold a candle to the Sheraton, where the intra-Afghan dialogue was supposed to have taken place. Prior to the conference, Barakat had requested of the Afghans that they not arrange any meetings with the Taliban in the Sheraton due to "diplomatic sensitivities." After a short drive, the exiled Afghans filed out of the bus and were received right on the street by a man with a full white beard, a black turban, and large sunglasses. Sher Mohammad Abbas Stanekzai was none other than the leader of the Taliban delegation in Qatar at the time. Other familiar faces had gathered behind him, such as Mohammad Sohail Shaheen, the group's spokesperson and media man, and Khairullah Khairkhwa, a former Guantánamo inmate who had been released and returned to Qatar as part of the controversial 2014 deal to secure the release of the US soldier Bowe Bergdahl. The Taliban led their guests into a large hotel lobby that appeared to have been reserved for the occasion, and exiled Afghans were seated. The focus of the seating arrangement was the only two women present, Khatol Mohmand, a journalist from Sweden (who is not related to Abdul Kadir Mohmand), and Masuda Sultan, an activist from the United States.

The Taliban know that their misogynistic attitude is viewed critically not only by the international community but also by many Afghans. Under the Taliban regime in the 1990s, women were effectively second-class citizens. In many regions, they were barred in practice from any form of work or education. Since the extremists have once again returned to the geopolitical spotlight, they have claimed time and again that they are not "against women." Along these lines, the Taliban leader Stanekzai has said that all Afghans, read, men *and* women, need to have their rights protected. At the same time, he has also made clear that the rights of which he speaks are those of an "Islamic governmental system." Hence, he has claimed that "Whoever wants a Western model of women's rights is in the wrong place. We aren't in the West but Afghanistan. We have our own customs and values." Prior to September 2021, Stanekzai and other Taliban leaders refused to specify what Islamic values would look like in a future Taliban emirate. That being said, the extremists did give the impression that they sought to impose their value system not only in the country's generally staunchly conservative rural regions, where they would likely meet little resistance, but also in major cities such as Kabul. Yet even in Afghanistan's villages, the Taliban model will not work in the long term. After all, these places as well are home to numerous people who are not willing to give up their new, hard-fought freedoms. The best example of this are the students of Habib ur-Rahman's girls' school in Khost. In Qatar, however, Sultan and Mohmand were surprised by the openness of the Taliban. In comparison to the men present, the women were—probably deliberately—granted an unusually long amount of speaking time, a circumstance they had not been counting on.

Nevertheless, during the conversation between the exiled Afghans and the Taliban, the developments of the coming months already became clear. In spite of the intensely one-sided worldview and total lack of solutions of the extremists and war criminals, their guests had a hard time contradicting them. For years, the Taliban had doggedly attacked every single failure of the Afghan government and its allies, highlighting the widespread corruption, flourishing drug trade, countless human rights abuses, and privileged lifestyles of many members of government. All the while, the Taliban's rhetoric had disguised the fact that they themselves were being implicated in a number of these matters. The extremists also had a number of dubious connections to governments and intelligence agencies and in particular to those of Pakistan and Iran, two countries that have spent decades fueling and exploiting the conflicts in Afghanistan. Yet once the withdrawal deal between the Taliban and the Trump administration was signed in Doha in late February 2020, the group found itself in a better position than ever before. Its members, self-identified resistance fighters, believed they had forced another empire to bend the knee. Ironically, this narrative was also encouraged by Washington.

During the Qatar negotiations between the Americans and the Taliban, the Afghan government under Ghani was systematically excluded. In the Taliban camp, the general attitude had been something along the lines of, "We won't talk to the puppets. We'll talk to the puppet masters," and Washington complied with this demand. The treaty with the extremists further underscored the Americans' appeasement. Above all, they had demanded that the Taliban not shelter groups such as Al Qaeda and ISIS. Shortly after the deal had been signed, reports circulated about US air strikes against ISIS in Kunar Province that had been tactically coordinated with and even strategically benefited the Taliban.[124] It also became clear that the group, which had largely profited from the war, did not simply want it to end—it wanted to be the one to bring order to the chaos. Yet it lacked a long-term strategy to this end. Many of the areas under Taliban control at the time were already suffering in multiple respects: the extremists had no idea how to govern, and they were incapable of providing for the fundamental needs of the population. Instead, they were trying to create "Islam-compliant" cafés and athletic clubs, as was reported by journalists such as Fazelminallah Qazizai, a native of the southern Helmand Province. Moreover, the difference in thinking between Taliban leaders on certain issues was noticeable. While the Americans and their allies in Kabul were treated with intransigence by Stanekzai, a different line was taken by Khairullah Khairkhwa, who had endured years of imprisonment and torture in Guantánamo. "We don't want the Americans to simply leave. They're the ones responsible for the current malaise, and they must recognize this," he told me back in April 2019. The fact that an ex-Guantánamo detainee of all people should offer such a realistic analysis astounded me.

Particularly critical of the Taliban, on the other hand, was the very man who once ran their mediation office in Qatar, Sayed Muhammad Tayyab Agha. In 2015, Agha had distanced himself from the group after it came out that multiple Taliban leaders had spent years concealing the death of its founder, Mullah Mohammad Omar. Back in the early years, Agha had served as secretary to Omar. "Afghan civil society and the Afghan diaspora need to make it clear to the Taliban delegation in Qatar that nothing will move forward without them," Agha told several exiled Afghans in his house in Doha. Time and again, rumors circulate that Agha had a falling out with older Taliban leaders over various disagreements. Among other things, these concerned the future of the Afghan army—many Taliban leaders had maintained that it would collapse if they recaptured the country, which eventually turned out to be true—as well as Pakistan's influence on the group, which Agha vehemently opposed.

Following the treaty, a saying had spread through Afghanistan that the only safe place from Taliban attacks was the shadow of an American military base. Attacks on Afghan army personnel, police officers, and civilians had continued apace. Many Afghans in Kabul now feared a repeat of the scenario that unfolded following the fall of Afghanistan's last Communist dictator, Mohammad Najibullah. In 1989, the last Soviet soldier left Afghanistan, and three years later, financial support from Moscow dried up. In 1992, the mujahideen rebels took the Afghan capital.

At the time of the would-be intra-Afghan dialogue in Doha, it was still unclear how long Washington planned to stand by its allies in Kabul. "You are a tough people," Donald Trump said in his first phone call with Mullah Abdul Ghani Baradar, the leader of the Taliban delegation in Qatar. The conversation was left out the White House records. The first reports of it were spread by the Taliban.[125] By all appearances, Trump maintained a better relationship with the leader of the Taliban than with his ally in Kabul, President Ashraf Ghani. Observers attributed this to Trump's personality, claiming the former president got along better with political strongmen. Yet Trump's approach has been continued by his successor, Joe Biden. Mere weeks after taking office, his administration made clear that it would not only follow through with the planned troop withdrawal but also do nothing to improve its frosty relationship with the Kabul government. But perhaps this was bound to happen, for Washington had long been soured on the actions of its allies in Kabul.

The Afghanistan Papers: The Bombshell That Wasn't

In late 2019, the *Washington Post* published "The Afghanistan Papers," a 2,000-page report showing that the 2001 NATO intervention in Afghanistan and everything that followed had been a complete mess. As Douglas Lute, war czar to Bush and Obama, is quoted therein, "We were devoid of a fundamental understanding of Afghanistan— we didn't know what we were doing [...]. We didn't have the foggiest notion of what we were undertaking." Similar sentiments can be found throughout the report, the product of more than 400 interviews with various insiders including leading military personnel and politicians. All of these figures more or less admitted that the War on Terror in Afghanistan was an unprecedented train wreck, and not one appeared to have any idea of how the dilemma might be solved. Several claimed that it had been common practice in the US command headquarters in Kabul to whitewash the war, to delude the public into thinking that victory over the Taliban was imminent. This narrative was pushed constantly, even when it was diametrically opposed to reality. According to the US army colonel Bob Crowley, all of the data that was shared with the Western public had been manipulated in order to paint as rosy an image of the war as possible. The report also contained an unambiguous if not unproblematic statement from the US diplomat James Dobbins: "We don't invade poor countries to make them rich. We don't invade authoritarian countries to make them democratic. We invade violent countries to make them peaceful and we clearly failed in Afghanistan."

Even the late former secretary of state Donald Rumsfeld, one of the leading architects of the War on Terror, had a premonition of what might be in store for the United States. In a memo from 2002, Rumsfeld wrote, "We are never going to get the U.S. military out of Afghanistan unless we take care to see that there is something going on that will provide the stability that will be necessary for us to leave." The memo concludes with a single word: "Help!" Among the other problems it highlighted, the Afghanistan Papers made it clear that the US knew virtually nothing about the "enemy." Had the Americans been fighting Al Qaeda, the Taliban, or other groups? And what was this enemy's actual presence over the years? Until 2021, the US military and the Kabul government claimed they were fighting Al Qaeda in Afghanistan, though no one could say exactly how many fighters the group had.

In 2014, I took part for the first time in the annual Afghanistan conference of the *Evangelische Akademie Villigst* in Schwerte, Germany. Also in attendance was Kay Brinkmann, a German brigadier general who had spent a lengthy deployment in Afghanistan and been invited to deliver a lecture. During his talk, Brinkmann displayed a map with the locations of various "enemies," including Al Qaeda. Yet when the German Afghanistan expert Thomas Ruttig asked Brinkmann whether there were 30, 300, or 3,000 Al Qaeda fighters in the country, the general began to stutter and couldn't give an answer. Similar responses to this question can be seen throughout the Afghanistan Papers from those interviewed. Though they may have been some of NATO's most powerful political and military decision-makers, they apparently had no idea what was happening in the country. Just as they could give few details about their "enemies," they also seemed to know little about the "friends" with whom they had allied on the ground. When the US invaded Afghanistan, the Americans primarily supported the corrupt politicians and brutal warlords who had rallied around Hamid Karzai. Many of them, including members of Karzai's own family, soon began using the millions of dollars they received to pursue their own agendas. They staged attacks to secure treaties with NATO troops, and they used US funding to break into the drug business.

Millions in aid money that could have gone towards modernizing virtually all of Afghanistan simply vanished. Whereas Afghan opium production had been virtually nonexistent at the time of the NATO invasion, the country became a top exporter of the crop.

Ahmed Wali Karzai, the brother of Hamid Karzai who was killed in 2011, rose to become one of Afghanistan's most important drug kingpins—and was on the CIA's payroll all the while, as were various other drug lords. Eventually, there were virtually no political actors in Afghanistan who were not involved in the drug trade in one form or the other. For its own part, the West pretended to have nothing to do with all this. And though new headlines about Afghan opium production reaching record highs appeared year after year during the war, seldom did the media actually contextualize or provide any kind of detailed analysis of this trend. Instead, the problem was "Afghanized," viewed in isolation, and typically blamed on the usual suspects. The authorities in Washington and elsewhere knew that the situation on the ground was complicated and would cast them in a negative light. After all, it was mainly their own allies who were driving the drug trade. There were even some reports that the West was participating extensively in the trade, just as the CIA had done in South America. In practice, this would mean that the West bears direct responsibility not only for the massive drug problem in Afghan society—where there are an estimated 4.5 million drug addicts—but also for increasing drug use among Western youth. Eighty percent of the world's heroin supply now comes from Afghanistan, a figure that applies on both European and Americans streets. Yet this and other realities mostly remain hidden in the West. Rather than admit their mistakes, the US and their allies preferred to deliberately deceive the public.

The man behind what eventually became known as the Afghan Papers was John Sopko, the US's Special Inspector General for Afghanistan Reconstruction (SIGAR). Tasked with getting to the bottom of this disaster of a war, he regularly published SIGAR reports for the US Congress. Everyone who was familiar with them knew how critical Sopko and his employees were in their approach. They did not seem mince words, a welcome surprise for many Afghanistan experts. However, once the reports that comprised the Afghan Papers began to be published in 2015, this impression was disappointed. They had been censored, the particularly critical statements they contained omitted. They were also supposed to remain under lock and key, but the *Washington Post* eventually forced the release of the ostensible bombshell thanks to the Freedom of Information Act and a three-year lawsuit.[126]

The Afghan Papers make it clear that war was intensely whitewashed. The primary victims of these PR efforts were not American soldiers or taxpayers but the Afghan population. Over the course of its twenty long years, the NATO occupation of Afghanistan was replete with plunder, torture, and murder. As we now know, it also involved copious and persistent lying. Yet was this really news? Were the Afghan Papers really "huge" or "a bombshell?" Those who had spent years following and vehemently criticizing the war knew that this was hardly the case. Once the report was published, there suddenly appeared a new consensus that the war in Afghanistan was going poorly, that it had indeed been going poorly for some time, but that people simply hadn't known. Sopko rejected this interpretation. In an opinion piece in the *Washington Post*, he emphasized the importance of the Afghan Papers' publication while also criticizing the newspaper's sensationalism, arguing that most of the facts it contained had not been "secret." Anyone who had carefully read the regular SIGAR reports would have reached similar conclusions a long time ago. Moreover, Sopko suggested that the Afghan Papers (or rather, the journalists who had compiled and edited them) ignored or disregarded the efforts of his team, who often worked under extremely difficult and dangerous conditions in Afghanistan. He also noted that in 2017 and 2018, the *Washington Post* refused to publish important SIGAR findings, even though he and his team had approached the editors with them.[127]

From the Afghan perspective, Europe and the United States are far too slow on the uptake when it comes to critical developments of this sort. "The experts in the West always realize their mistakes far too late. Only after a few years do they say, 'Oh, the others were right,'" Waheed Mozhdah said, who was expressly mentioned at the beginning of this book. After the fall of the Taliban regime,

Mozhdah focused on his work as a writer, political analyst, and peace activist. He was one of the harshest critics of the Western occupation and the corrupt power apparatus that ruled in Kabul for its duration. In December 2019, Mozhdah was murdered in front of his house in Kabul by a man on a motorcycle wielding a pistol with a silencer. His burial and funeral were attended by thousands, including figures of various political stripes. Former president Hamid Karzai was present, as were representatives of the Taliban, the mujahideen, and the Communist PDPA, as well as members of minority groups such as the Shia Hazara. "One saw Communists, Islamists, liberals, and nationalists, all of whom had gathered together to pay this man their last respects," one of the guests later remarked in an interview. "Mozhdad stood for freedom and unity. He transcended political borders, parties, and worldviews."

I myself was connected to Mozhdah, not only professionally but personally. He was my uncle, the oldest brother of my mother. Every day during my trips to Afghanistan, I saw how he was constantly sought out by Western journalists, analysts, and NGO workers. Western embassies invited him to educate them about Afghanistan. Those who came to pay him a visit and hear him speak valued his expertise, positively soaking it up, with Mozhdah always taking enough time to answer all questions. He was also a frequent guest on Afghan talk shows and held reading and lectures in Kabul. There is virtually no Afghanistan expert who has not cited him at least once. In 2013, Mozhdah's critical stance towards the powerful made him the target of a politically motivated media campaign. After criticizing the bilateral security agreement with the US as a "colonial pact," he was slandered and denounced as an "agent of the Taliban" and a "traitor," though he regularly criticized the Taliban and the mujahideen, both of whom he had once served. The focus of the media campaign was a phone call between Mozhdah and an alleged Taliban member, which had been recorded by the Afghan intelligence agency NDS and released in response to pressure from Rangin Dadfar Spanta, a former foreign minister of the Karzai government.

Spanta had once received asylum in Germany, where he was involved in in local politics for years as a member of Germany's Green Party.

The accusations against Mozhdah were quickly debunked; the NDS merely interrogated him and drove him home, and many experts on the conflict knew that his peace activism meant that he maintained contact with almost all war parties, including the Taliban. However, the campaign permanently damaged Mozhdah's reputation—and probably also led to his eventual murder. During his burial ceremony, Spanta approached Mozhdah's family and apologized for the mistake he had committed out of selfishness and lust for power. Yet it was too late for apologies. In the final years of the NATO occupation, critics of it and of the Kabul government such as Mozhdah were sometimes consciously hunted down, murdered, and exiled. Critics placed most of the blame for this on the very forces that had been singled out for support and brought to power by Washington and its allies from late 2001 onward, and especially on the shadowy actors within NDS.[128]

As the Afghan Papers made clear, local experts such as Mozhdah were almost entirely disregarded during the two decades of occupation. The occupiers were fundamentally uninterested in their critical observations. The result of this approach could not have been more disastrous. When the original German version of this book was being written, the Afghanistan War was in its twentieth year, and chaos and destruction still reigned. Alone in the time it took to write, numerous districts in northern Afghanistan were captured by the Taliban. Meanwhile, the Bundeswehr withdrew from the country, and the US military left Bagram, the central hub of the War on Terror in Afghanistan, in a cloak-and-dagger operation. The West's Afghan warlords also made haste.

US media outlets began to report that over 43,000 Afghan civilians had been killed in the course of the war. This too must be regarded as an absolute low-end estimate. The number of unrecorded deaths is likely many times higher. Meanwhile, the American public in particular might be shocked to know that, while 2,400 US soldiers were killed in the Hindu Kush, this figure pales in comparison to the number of soldiers who have committed suicide since the start of the War on Terror: according to an extensive report published in June 2021, at least 30,177 US soldiers have taken their own lives since the September 11 attacks. All in all, the wars in Iraq, Afghanistan, and elsewhere had claimed the lives of over 7,000 soldiers and cost Washington 1.5 trillion dollars as of 2021, including 500 billion in interest alone. The rest was "invested" in Afghanistan, though there's no question that most of this money was siphoned off. It not only fueled corruption in the country but made it possible in the first place.

At the Front in the Pech Valley

Hamza Mohammadi is a man in his early twenties with dark blond hair and a full beard. He is wearing sneakers with his military uniform. As the young soldier smiles at the camera and poses with his weapon next to a rubbernecker, shots ring out in the background. A few meters away, two Afghan army Humvees target a barely visible Taliban position high up in the mountains, one of many in the Pech Valley in Kunar. The chaos of the skirmish has caused a traffic jam on the road to the neighboring province of Nooristan, a place not easy to access under normal circumstances. The soldiers fire their salvos at irregular intervals. Nothing of the enemy can be seen or heard. "They're hiding up there," a soldier hisses.

Shortly before, a landmine had exploded along the road. The Taliban were targeting the entourage of a local warlord by the name of Commander Matiullah, whose son had been killed the night before. The entourage was heading to his funeral. Now the task of repairing the damaged road has fallen to the civilians trying to pass, who have nothing to do with all of the conflicts between government troops, warlords, and the Taliban. They attempt to fill the small crater in the ground with rocks while observing the fighting as it unfolds. Some people drink tea, take pictures of the landscape, or talk loudly with friends and relatives. The whole situation feels surreal. However, scenes such as this one have become all too normal in a country where war has reigned and determined everyday life for more than forty years.

This scene took place following the agreed withdrawal of NATO troops. The agreement did nothing to stem the skirmishes in Afghanistan, which continued to produce ever more civilian casualties. According to the UNAMA report from April 2021, the first quarter of that year saw at least 573 civilians killed and 1,210 injured.[129] The death toll among security forces was typically much higher, though it was seldom accounted for. Many of the soldiers were young men like Mohammadi—and they were left to fend for themselves following the NATO withdrawal. This was obvious above all in regions such as the Pech Valley. *Pech* (pronounced "paitsch") means "screw." The valley is famous for its winding streets and rivers—and for its guerrilla warfare. Back in the 1980s, the mujahideen rebels successfully fought the Red Army here, shooting down Soviet helicopters. Years later, numerous elite soldiers of the US army would also discover with the perils of the Pech Valley. They would see that it was almost as if the valley had been created for guerrilla war. As soon as the combat helicopters of the US military entered, fighters could hear them due to the numerous ravines and mountains—and prepare themselves accordingly. Much of the population of the Pech Valley is not only traditional Sunni but also Salafi, as can be seen from the numerous nameless gravestones in its graveyards. Non-Muslim invaders are thus viewed all the more resolutely as enemies who must be fought.

The eponymous Pech District is also home to the famous Korengal Valley, which made it into US pop culture years ago through documentary films such as *Restrepo* and *Korengal*. Ten kilometers in length and five in width, the valley serves as a good encapsulation of the American failure in Afghanistan. US troops deserted it as early as 2013. This delighted the local population: many of the people with whom I spoke made no secret of their contempt for the foreign troops, proudly pointing out the empty bases in the area. "It is good that these oppressors are gone. God is great," a young man from Pech Valley told me. This sentiment is hardly surprising. In Kunar, US bombings and brutal night raids had been part of everyday life.

During those days, the journalist Wesley Morgan produced remarkable reportage from the region. Accompanying the American troops as a so-called embedded reporter, he interviewed many of the soldiers stationed in Kunar. Among other things, Morgan described how after Taliban ambushes, the troops would take out their anger on civilians through gratuitous raids, torture, and bombings based on faulty information. In true wild west fashion, some US soldiers even stormed the bazaar in Asadabad, whereas others furiously confronted locals and tried to order them around without an interpreter. "A young boy laughed at them," Morgan recalled. The locals probably made the Americans feel like the attacks on them had been justified. A particularly harrowing example of the Americans' unfathomable behavior can be seen in the former CIA agent David Passaro, who was fond of "interrogating" "terror suspects" with various torture methods. One of them was Abdul Wali, a respected local man whom the sadistic Passaro arrested, tortured, and murdered in June 2003. The news of his death spread throughout the province. According to US military testimony, Passaro was a bad apple who was despised by his colleagues. Yet to most Afghans in Kunar, men like him were far closer to the rule than an exception. Back in the US, Passaro was sentenced to eight years in prison, making him the only CIA agent since the start of the War on Terror to have been legally prosecuted for his crimes. According to former Kunar governor Said Fazal Akbar, Passaro's murder of the innocent Abdul Wali was a key factor in strengthening the Taliban in the region.[130]

Yet even the withdrawal of US troops did not bring peace to Kunar. In addition to the Taliban, both Al Qaeda and ISIS had a presence in the province. After the American soldiers had left, the war continued to be waged on the backs of the Afghan people. "We've fought for a long time, and with God's help, we will win," Mohammadi told me. Originally from the Dar-e Noor District in the bordering Nangarhar Province, he had been stationed in Pech Valley for several months when we spoke. At the time, he could only visit his family at irregular intervals. Mohammadi was unfazed by the Americans' abandonment Kunar and other locations. "This here is our fight. We need to sort it out ourselves," he said. Abdul Hadi, another soldier and brother-in-arms of Mohammadi, is more skeptical. "Look around here. This is our daily life. How long is this supposed to go on?" he asked. A native of Kabul, Abdul Hadi had never been to other Afghan provinces before becoming a soldier. "Life here is different than in Kabul. A lot of people, including the responsible politicians in charge, have no idea what's happening here," he said. Along with Mohammadi and the other soldiers, Abdul Hadi recently had to bury a fallen comrade. At the time, one seldom heard about all the Afghan army soldiers being killed daily in Afghanistan.

In September 2019, Donald Trump briefly called off peace talks with the Taliban after a US soldier was killed in a skirmish. "The talks are dead," Trump proclaimed shortly before the anniversary of the September 11 attacks. They were initiated again several weeks later by Washington. During that same time period, hundreds of Afghan soldiers were killed by the rebels. Most of them had been simple men from poor families, like Mohammadi and Abdul Hadi. The signing of the US-Taliban peace deal in Doha did nothing to change this. "The Americans have been gone for some time. But we can't leave. This is our country, and we are defending it," I was told by Sayyed Agha, a soldier stationed near the Pakistani border in Sarkano District.

His monthly salary was around $150. His border outpost was small and remote. There was no electricity, and the soldiers had to fetch water with canisters from high up on a nearby hill. Over the two decades of the war, billions of dollars flowed into the Afghan army. Detailed reports generally say that around $87 billion were invested in building up Afghan security forces. Yet the soldiers in Kunar lacked the most basic necessities. One reason for this was widespread corruption. High-ranking military officials personally enriched themselves while the men fighting at the front had virtually nothing. Often, they pocketed the salaries of soldiers who only existed on paper, leading observers to speak of "ghost soldiers." The soldiers who actually existed were typically left to their own devices. Their neglect and poor pay led to mass desertions, such as took place during the Taliban offensive in the summer of 2021. Following twenty years of NATO occupation, the Afghan army was a failed institution that the extremists ultimately toppled without much effort. Soldiers who surrendered were either humiliated or massacred. Sayyed Agha blamed the Kabul government for this. "We are fighting for politicians who have foreign citizenships. They would never send their own sons here," Agha complained. Even before the Taliban victory, the government of President Ashraf Ghani had long been criticized for having lost its connection to reality. Many of Ghani's closest advisors were Afghans based abroad, some of whom did not even speak any of the country's languages. Time and again, they made headlines for their involvement in corruption scandals. The situation at the front was of no interest to them. "These people are living in their own world, and this world has nothing in common with ours. We're not fighting for them. We're fighting for our country," Agha mused. He then grabbed his canister and headed up the hill.

Quo vadis, Afghanistan?

THE ORIGINAL GERMAN edition of this book appeared shortly before the twentieth anniversary of the attacks of September 11, 2001. At that time, Afghanistan had endured two decades of the War on Terror and more than forty years of war. The majority of Afghan society knows nothing other than conflict, chaos, and displacement. The generation that had the privilege to experience the time of freedom is shrinking every day. The trauma that members of that generation experienced can hardly be measured. Whenever I was at the Kabul airport, I always noticed how older people who were returning to their homeland for the first time in decades would break into tears upon encountering the dramatic changes and reigning conditions. My own father and several other members of my family have not been back to Afghanistan for more than forty years because they would not be able to bear the sight of their homeland—and because the country in which they were born no longer exists. Unfortunately, it is unlikely that the status quo in Afghanistan will change any time soon. The Western deployment has now failed. The Americans, the Germans, and the soldiers of other allied nations have finally withdrawn. Much of their military equipment was captured by the Taliban when hundreds of Afghan soldiers fled their posts during the extremists' offensive. During the war years, the Taliban not only developed new tactics but also appropriated the "achievements" of the War on Terror. They now use rudimentary armed drones and spread propaganda videos of their Red Unit, a Taliban special forces unit that can hardly be distinguished from its American counterparts. Meanwhile, the dark cloud that hovered over Kabul during the Taliban's final offensive has now broken. At the time, many Afghans though that it was only a question of time until the Taliban took the capital, and they were proven right. "You have the clocks, but we have the time," is an old saying in Afghanistan. In the final years of the war, Western observers often attributed this saying to the Taliban, and indeed, it was a fairly apt summation of the events in the Hindu Kush. By all appearances, time had run out for the Western troops. Now, it was the Afghans who were fighting among themselves. The War on Terror was almost completely "Afghanized"—and in many cases, it was a civil war. Families joined different political camps and declared each other the enemy. Mourning mothers buried their sons, some of whom had been clothed in black Taliban turbans, others in the Afghan army uniform. This is the real tragedy of war, and this tragedy does not appear to want to run its course.

Though the Taliban have now recaptured Afghanistan, it should now be obvious to everyone involved that the deep-seated divisions in the Hindu Kush can only be reconciled with words as opposed to weapons. There were moments of hope during the war that made this clear. Cease-fires between the war parties always took place during the Islamic Feast of the Sacrifice. During the feast days, both Taliban fighters and soldiers of the Afghan army laid down their weapons and broke bread together, and they were able to visit their families in peace. "Why not a Feast of the Sacrifice all the time?" I asked both young Taliban fighters in Baghlan Province and their political leadership in Qatar. Just like the political elite and the high-ranking military officers in Kabul, they could not answer my question. Both sides preferred to blame the other and double down on their nationalist or Islamist ideologies—which I suspect carry little appeal for most of the population. Diversity of opinion and political position have always existed in Afghanistan.

At one time—in my grandparents' day, for example—there was a vibrant culture of debate. People with contrasting beliefs could still be good friends. In the 1960s and 1970s, nationalists, Islamists, leftists, Communists, and liberals would meet in my grandfather's living room in Kabul to discuss the affairs of their country. In this book, we have repeatedly shown that this era was far from perfect, yet the positive developments to which it bore witness must not be forgotten. This is by no means a question of nostalgia or historical revisionism. Rather, the memory of this era is important for promoting a new intra-Afghan reconciliation. Among the general population, this reconciliation has been ongoing for some time. An especially praiseworthy example can be seen near the Kabul bazaar. There, Shams ul-Haqq, my bookseller of choice, has worked side by side for more than twenty-five years with his friend and former "archenemy" Hajji Sherazuddin.

Together, the two men have experienced the fall and rise of various governments. Earlier, they had fought each other, albeit indirectly: while Shams ul-Haqq was working for the military intelligence agency of the Communist regime in Kabul during the Cold War, a young Sherazuddin was fighting on the side of the mujahideen rebels. "The guy was bashing in Russian skulls back then. Hard to believe, right?" the white-bearded Shams ul-Haqq told me jokingly during my last visit to his book stand. Sporting his trademark pakol hat and grim expression, Sherazuddin broke into a grin. He was once ideologically committed to armed jihad against the Soviet troops. "They attacked us. We were just defending ourselves," he said. In spite of working for the other side at the time, Shams ul-Haqq now shares his colleague's opinion. "I wasn't a Communist. The situation was complicated, but in the end, it was good that the Soviets withdrew," he said. However, he wasn't quite sure what to think about the impending withdrawal of the NATO troops. "It's a dilemma—with or without them!" he summed up. Hajji Sherazuddin saw things differently.

He thought the foreign troops needed to leave. They had only brought suffering to Afghanistan, he claimed with his pointer finger raised in the air. While Hajji Sherazuddin mainly sells textbooks to students, Shams ul-Haqq offers mainly nonfiction books and political autobiographies. Alongside the Persian translations of Che Guevara's diaries and Hitler's *Mein Kampf,* one can spot the visages of the same men who have shaped Afghanistan in recent years: Mohammad Daoud Khan, the first and last president of the Afghan republic, the mujahideen leader Ahmad Shah Massoud, and Mohammad Najibullah, the man who ruled Afghanistan as its last Soviet-backed Communist dictator before his brutal execution by the Taliban. "All in all, they've all destroyed our country," ul-Haqq remarked cynically.

He is not the type to romanticize Afghanistan's history. To him, all of the political leaders of the past years have blood on their hands, and they have been blindly followed by men such as himself, who once celebrated the Communist coup that was the 1978 Saur Revolution, and the former mujahideen Hajji Sherazuddin. Now is the time for this to come to an end, ul-Haqq said. "If we can make peace, anyone can," he remarked euphorically, as Sherazuddin nodded affirmatively. "The political leaders on both sides need to take advantage of this important moment and make peace," he added. This goes to show that an intra-Afghan peace from below has long been in the making. Yet even after the Afghanistan War has ended, conflict is being perpetuated by political leaders unwilling to part ways with their influence and profiteering. Genuine dialogue, reconciliation, and confrontation of wartime atrocities would challenge the status of these very actors and possibly force them to answer for their actions—hopefully (!) in front of an independent Afghan court that sentences perpetrators to prison and not the torture chamber.

Retro Perspective: America's failure, explained by one village

Mussahi District, Kabul Province, March 2019: A small group of men and boredom-prone children stand by the riverside. All of them stare at the contraption before them: a small water pump that, despite their best efforts, won't turn on. A young man tries to set it in motion by pushing at the gear and pulling at the engine, all the while concentrating on the tube protruding from the lifeless pump. The water in the river remains still and calm. The pump, sent by a relative who spent the last two decades in Germany, simply won't work. It's an all too typical story in Mussahi, 30 kilometers (around 19 miles) south of the capital itself, where, for as long as memory recalls, many things have not functioned. Much like Mussahi's water pump, most of Afghanistan doesn't function either, at least outside the major cities. And even if the then newly reelected president, Ashraf Ghani, did his best to try to improve things, he would have a hard time holding off the Taliban.

Eighteen years after the US-led invasion of Afghanistan, the capital city of Kabul has undergone several transformations. The city is dotted with high-rises that fill the skyline. Roads are slowly, and painstakingly, being paved. The monuments of eras gone by are being renovated. A small moneyed class, cosmopolitan and more connected with other global capitals than the countryside a mere drive away, fuels the slow growth of Western-style coffee shops across the city, complete with increasingly popular one-dollar lattes. More than half of the country's population, meanwhile, lives on less than one dollar a day. The transformation is topped off with mansions and fancy wedding halls: effectively barricaded compounds where urban elites display obscene wealth. The dystopian picture is complete with a short drive south of the city, wherein lies a different world: a world left behind and pummeled by years of poverty and war. Mussahi has been a part of Kabul Province for decades now, but in 2019, it is part of a growing area of Kabul's outskirts falling under a steadily darkening Taliban shadow. Although not visible during the day, the fall of darkness is accompanied by them erecting their checkpoints. This reality has not and will not change, even after the release of the final results of what ended up being the occupation era's last presidential elections. After five months of waiting, Ashraf Ghani has been declared the winner. His rival is the former foreign minister Abdullah Abdullah, who had also contested him in 2014's elections. In 2014 too, Abdullah had disputed the results of elections that were widely agreed to be fraudulent; he was only pacified through a US-brokered power sharing agreement that made him the national unity government's chief executive, a position created just for him, and like much of the government's machinery, without legal or constitutional basis. Despite the theatrics, no doubt entertaining for many, Abdullah and Ghani (and soon enough the Republic they were leaders of) have lost support in rural places like Mussahi. During their presidential election campaigns, while the political elites in the city celebrated their much-touted but hollow democracy, the people of Mussahi were shut out from the political process entirely. The Taliban's predominance precluded travel into the capital and the resultant opportunity to engage the candidates directly during their live televised interviews. Conversely, it also precluded the possibility of the candidates being able to campaign or even visit what was a district of Kabul. On Election Day, the very real threat of Taliban attack meant the polling stations remained closed. The signs of failure are written all over Mussahi, and many residents, unsurprisingly, express their dissatisfaction with the nation's leadership. Many also vocally support the Taliban. Within the district, soldiers of the Afghan National Army, created and trained by the US and its allies after 2001, are disregarded. The war was, in many respects, lost before it was fought; soldiers knew that it was Taliban country. Entering it would needlessly risk their lives. Few of them appear periodically for Friday prayers. When they do, they look insecure and nervous. As it turned out, they knew, perhaps better than even the Taliban, that the war was lost.

"They just want to leave as soon as possible. They know that nobody wants to see them here," said a resident. The truth was that few soldiers, if any, could make it past their marked checkpoint on the bridge that marked the entrance to the district itself. Several residents I spoke to then complained about corrupt local government officials and voiced support for the Taliban. Unlike government officials, they argued, the Taliban actually got things done. For instance, long standing family-feuds, common across the country, are finally being resolved in Taliban courts. "This is [the Taliban's] court. They have the control here," says a local who wanted to remain unnamed. Many rural districts in Afghanistan are already fully controlled by or under the influence of the Taliban. According to various estimates from that time, more than half of the country is contested or controlled by them.

This reality had been, and remains, largely ignored in both Washington and Kabul. Instead, the US government tried to paint a different picture of the war, one dominated by (white) lies, omissions, and exaggerations. Mussahi, barely a stone's throw from the nation's capital, is a prime example of exactly what went wrong over twenty years. Washington had poured more than $2 trillion into the country, without much to show for it. The only "aid" that could be found in Mussahi is a defective German water pump from the 1950s, when the country was ruled by a monarchy that enjoyed relations with Germany and its two governments on either side of the Berlin Wall.

"There has not been any other aid. We have many problems here, especially with farming. But as you can see, we have to figure out how this pump works. It is sad that we remained that backward, but nobody is interested in our cause," said Mohammad Azif, a farmer from a village in the district. Like many other Afghans, Azif hopes that peace talks with the Taliban will be successful. He and his fellow villagers, at long last, could just focus on rebuilding their homes. "We can live in poverty but not without peace. We cannot move freely at night. There is always fighting between the army and the insurgents. We need a peace deal that serves the interests of all Afghans," he underlined. Mohammad Shaheen, who lives in Kabul but visits Mussahi regularly with his family, believes that the government would continue to be careless about the daily problems of the villagers. "This is the closest district to the capital. The presidential palace is [only] 15 kilometers from here, but we have so many problems here in terms of economy and security. The government does not care," he says. Mussahi might have been a short drive from the palace, a part of the province both the president and chief executive have resided in for decades, but the people there continue to feel politically helpless.

Mussahi is just one example out of many. Often, it appears as though rural Afghanistan does not exist in the minds of many urbanites. In some respects, this wasn't entirely new. Especially in Kabul, political elites had always lived in their own bubble. When the British twice invaded Afghanistan in the nineteenth century, their installed monarchs ruled in Kabul as rural Afghans organized resistance. When the Soviets invaded the country in 1979, people in the cities benefited, often handsomely, from housing projects and infrastructure. Hundreds of villages, meanwhile, were wiped off the map by the Soviet Red Army and its Afghan Communist allies.

The government of Ashraf Ghani, today mainly known as Afghanistan's runaway president who left the country after the Taliban returned on August 15, 2021, was not able to change these long-standing realities. Instead, the Western-backed regime subsumed that attitude and took it to astronomical heights. Ghani's government largely consisted of Westernized technocrats, often with dual citizenships, often unable to speak the local languages but prized for their impressive Western degrees. This could be observed in every aspect of life. In the context of ongoing peace talks with the Taliban, for example, many rural Afghans like those in Mussahi welcomed any kind of violence reduction and appeared optimistic, while large parts of the country's urban elites feared for their lucrative and powerful positions.

As of August 2019, Ghani celebrates the 100th anniversary of Afghanistan's independence in Kabul's newly renovated Dar-ul-Aman palace. American air strikes and night raids conducted by CIA-backed Afghan militias, concurrently, have dramatically increased in the country's rural areas. At the same time, insurgent violence escalated and large parts of the country were under Taliban control. Last but not least, Ghani's entire government was and remains dependent on economic and military aid from the US and its allies. To many Afghans, it appeared more than paradoxical to celebrate an alleged independence under such circumstances. However, many, both Afghans and non-Afghans, have no idea how haunting the realities of Mussahi and many other rural regions of the country would become, and that in the end, everything would collapse.

Epilogue: Checkpoint realities

"AFGHANISTAN IS LIKE a cage at the moment," says Sameh ur-Rahman. "We truly hope that it changes very soon." During the late 1970s and 1980s, Sameh served as a colonel in the army of the People's Democratic Party of Afghanistan, the Afghan Communists. He lost his leg fighting the mujahideen. With the departure of the final Soviet troops in 1989, he had hoped that war would finally end, and the country could focus on prospering and healing as a society. Three decades later, and after the withdrawal of another superpower, his optimism has waned. Some of Colonel Sameh's children live in Europe; those in Afghanistan intend to leave. "There is nothing left here," his son-in-law Zahed tells me. It is not just Kabul that has changed. When I visited Afghanistan the first time after the Taliban takeover, the group's checkpoints controlled every corner, bringing an uneasy but rare calm to the country. These armed and bearded men are still an unfamiliar sight for Afghans in the capital. During the past twenty years, many residents never left the city but heard horror stories about the 1990s Taliban emirate and the current generation of insurgents who were fighting the American occupation. For many, violent savagery is personified by the figure of the bearded man with the dark turban, whose rage Kabul occasionally experienced as bombings and suicide attacks.

My friends and relatives seemed intimidated by Taliban checkpoints. Among other things, they face language barriers. The ethnically heterogeneous Kabulis primarily speak Farsi; the majority of the Taliban are rural Pashtuns who speak Pashto. The intelligibility of their Pashto depends on their provincial and tribal backgrounds; some dialects are incomprehensible even to fellow Pashtuns. A culture gap and mutual suspicion stymie any friendly exchange between urban residents and the fighters who had routinely struck their cities and now rule them. After twenty years of war and occupation, Afghanistan is largely at peace but ruled by what cannot as yet be considered a government. The Taliban are more an armed militia that has seized the reins of state—an armed militia ill-acquainted with the mechanisms of statecraft and the norms of diplomacy, with little sense of the domestic or international implications of their actions. "I will leave very soon," Sayyed Munawar, a Kabuli in his early sixties, told me when I saw him in spring 2022. "There is no future here." For the past fifteen years, he had worked for a well-known NGO. Now he lives in Iran with his wife and two daughters; his sons left for Europe months before the Taliban's return. For Munawar and other Afghans, it's not just the Taliban's incompetence but the way in which the group's ideologues keep conjuring ways to interfere in people's private lives that is so suffocating.

I got a taste of it myself on my way to Bamiyan with Munawar to see the Buddha statues and report on the Hazara minority's life under the Taliban. The car stereo was playing songs by the beloved Afghan singer Nashenas. A few moments before reaching the gates of Bamiyan, we turned off the music, a necessary precaution in Afghanistan under the Taliban. During its first rule, the group had banned music and destroyed cassettes. "They once stopped me at their checkpoint and wanted me to hand over my music cassettes," Munawar remembered. He decided to destroy them himself in front of the Talibs before giving what he considered his "treasure" to them. The cassettes have since been replaced by memory cards and smartphones, which are harder to police. The only music the Taliban fighters allow themselves are taranas, religious a cappella songs replete with references to jihad.

As I was trying to disconnect Munawar's phone from the stereo, he was distracted and stopped a few feet short of the Taliban checkpoint. That was a grave mistake. The fighters, who were already watching us, ran toward our car. "Get out!" they yelled while pointing their Kalashnikovs. "Calm down. No need to worry," I said. They wanted to search us. We did not resist and apologized for our error. The ordeal was far from over. Ahmad, another friend who was traveling with us, was forced by a young Talib to hand over his smartphone and open it for him. A few moments later, the fighter was checking Ahmad's photo gallery, featuring photos of his female family members, a gross violation of Afghan custom. "I got you," he suddenly yelled. "Now you are done!" He had found a TikTok video that he deemed immoral. The same happened to Munawar and his phone. Both were in a state of panic.

Incidents such as these are not uncommon. In recent months, the Taliban have increased their surveillance, and patrolling fighters often harass citizens, checking their phones. At the gates of Bamiyan, the Taliban next asked me to hand over my phone. I resisted. "That's similar to what the Americans did when they raided your houses," I said to an elder fighter. "Who the hell are you?" he asked me angrily. "Where are your documents?" I introduced myself as a journalist and showed him my German press card. His expression softened. "We don't have a problem with you," he said. It was Ahmad's phone that had "problematic" content, he said. After an hourlong discussion, the Taliban decided not to hand us over to their intelligence service, as they had threatened, and let us enter Bamiyan, albeit with a "guarantee." While Ahmad had to hand over his second phone, I was forced to leave my press card with them. "I will return it to you when you leave the province and go back to Kabul," their leader, who introduced himself as Qari Mohammad Daoud, told us.

While we were having breakfast in Bamiyan, both Munawar and Ahmad looked depressed. I knew that they had not had such an experience in a long time. Before the Taliban's return to power, travel in Afghanistan was difficult. On every journey, one had to navigate several checkpoints, from the local police to the army to intelligence militias to the Islamic State group. One had to prepare appropriate answers for each checkpoint to be able to get through. Many routes were inaccessible because of unending war among factions. This was the first time within years that we could travel to Bamiyan by car. The route was fraught with danger in the past because of the unstable situation in Maidan Wardak, a Taliban stronghold that lies between Kabul and Bamiyan. But now the Taliban rule alone, and the checkpoints are all theirs. For many Afghans this is a relief as they can travel the country safely for the very first time in their lives. Foreign reporters and vloggers have had much to say in recent months about the country's newfound "security." After four decades, most Afghans are tired of war. But few confuse security with "peace."

"These people, the Taliban, are not made to rule," says one friend. A mujahed who had fought the Soviets in the 1980s, he had earlier supported the Taliban's return, believing them to be an improvement of the corrupt previous government. Under both Hamid Karzai and Ashraf Ghani, the government was dominated by corrupt officials, and the Afghan Parliament turned into a bazaar where seats and positions were traded for millions of dollars. Instead of focusing on the people's needs, many politicians built ostentatious mansions, drove bulletproof cars, and siphoned stolen aid money off to Dubai. Reviled by many, most of them unsurprisingly fled Afghanistan. "God shamed these traitors," says the former mujahed. The Taliban, however, are hardly an improvement. Since August 2021, girls' high schools in most parts of the country remain closed. The only education allowed is under the strict banner of the Taliban, whose policies seem rooted in their own sexual anxieties. In most cases, younger women are not allowed to teach boys while younger men are not allowed to teach girls. "Appropriate" caps and "correct" hijabs have become part of the cities' new reality and are strictly enforced by the Taliban's moral police.

Some young Afghans are still resisting these constraints. "I love the perahan tunban, our traditional Afghan attire. But now I want to protest with my jeans and T-shirt in front of these guys," says Bezhan Karimi, a student at Kabul University. "It's as if we were not Muslims before," a female teacher from the northern city of Mazar-e Sharif tells me. While she worked several months without pay, she struggled with the Taliban authorities "because of ridiculous issues." She fears for the future of her daughters. "I cannot imagine them living and working here," she says. Afghanistan is a place full of contradictions. My father left the country to study in Europe more than four decades ago, before the Communist coup. He had grown up in an urban, elite family and learned German at the Amani High School, which was founded by Afghan King Amanullah. When I used to visit our local mosque in Austria on Eid wearing the perahan tunban, the Afghan attire Karimi mentioned, my father would joke by asking me why I was leaving the house in my pajamas. He grew up with suit pants and elegant shirts in 1960s Kabul. He despised the Communists (whose leaders used to visit my grandfather, a renowned intellectual and writer) for throwing his country into chaos. But my father also did not like the mullahs and clerics, who preached water but drank wine. The elites from different political factions often had close ties. Some of Afghanistan's leading Marxist and Islamist thinkers descended from the same families. Such paradoxes have endured. During the past twenty years of the US war, you would find one brother who joined the Taliban while another fought for the Afghan National Army. My father became a refugee in the aftermath of a brutal coup by the Afghan Communists in 1978. From the Soviet occupation to the Civil War in the 1990s and from the Taliban's first era to the invasion of the US and its allies, he has not returned to the country. After the Soviet invasion, my father busied himself with building a new life in Austria, where I was born. But though he left Afghanistan, Afghanistan never left him. The country he once knew does not exist anymore. Even the music he once listened to is now subject to an unofficial ban. I often wonder how he would react if he met today's rulers on the streets of

Kabul. Life in exile is permanently suspended between two worlds. And in many ways, it is the same for me and my siblings. "We are leaving" is a phrase I hear often when I visit my parents' country. But the question I always hesitate to ask, though I know the answer, is: "Will you ever arrive?"

Endnotes

1   Gary Younge: "Congresswoman Barbara Lee: once the lone voice against the Afghanistan war," July 27, 2012, online at theguardian.com.

2   See ZDF heute journal: "Afghanistan—Bundeswehr zu sanft (Uli Gack)," report from vom December 15, 2009, online at youtube.com.

3   See Michael Slackman, Greg Winter, Adrienne Carter & Doug Schorzman: "Our Next Kabul Bureau Chief," April 29, 2020, online at www.nytco.com.

4   Author interview with Erik Edstrom, November 2020.

5   See Michael Hirsh, "Bernard Lewis Revisited," November 1, 2004, online at washingtonmonthly.com.

6   See Fazelminallah Qazizai and Chris Sands, *Night Letters: Gulbuddin Hekmatyar and the Afghan Islamists Who Changed the World*, Hurst, 2019, p. 50.

7   Thomas Hegghammer, *The Caravan: Abdallah Azzam and the Rise of Global Jihad*, Cambridge UP, 2020, p. 17.

8   Hegghammer 2020, p. 98.

9   Fazelminallah Qazizai and Chris Sands, *Night Letters: Gulbuddin Hekmatyar and the Afghan Islamists Who Changed the World*, Hurst, 2019, p. 68.

10 Qazizai and Sands 2019, p. 213.

11 Author interview with Mohamedou Ould Slahi, 2017.

12 Abdullah Anas, *To the Mountains: My Life in Jihad, from Algeria to Afghanistan*, Hurst, 2019.

13 Aryn Baker, "Who Killed Abdullah Azzam?," *Time*, June 18, 2009, online at www.content.time.com.

14 Author's interviews with Mozhdah, 2014–2018.

15 Wahid Mozhdah, *Afghanistan Under Five Years of Taliban Rule*, 2002, p. 32; Reuters, "Man who brought al Qaeda to Afghanistan now runs for president," October 3, 2013, online at www.reuters.com.

16 Robert D. Crews, *Afghan Modern: The History of a Global Nation*, Harvard UP, 2015.

17 Niamatullah Ibrahimi, *The Hazara and the Afghan State: Rebellion, Exclusion and the Struggle for Recognition*, Hurst, 2017.

18 Bette Dam, *A Man and a Motorcycle: How Hamid Karzai Became Afghanistan's President*, Ipso Facto, 2014, p. 31.

19 Dam 2014, pp. 33ff.

20 Dam 2014, p. 32.

21 Bob Woodward, *Bush at War*, Simon & Schuster, 2002, p. 214.

22 Andy Worthington, *The Guantanamo Files: The Stories of 774 Detainees in America's Illegal Prison*, Pluto, 2007, pp. 22–3.

23 Worthington 2007, p. 19.

24 Kathy Gannon, "Kabul awakes to the aftermath of another night's heavy bombing," *The Guardian*, October 27, 2001, online at www.theguardian.com.

25   Human Rights Watch, *Blood-Stained Hands: Past Atrocities in Kabul and Afghanistan's Legacy of Impunity*, July 6, 2005, online at www.hrw.org.

26   Craig Murray, "Why the US won't admit it was jilted," *The Guardian*, August 3, 2005, online at www.theguardian.com.

27   Daveed Gartenstein-Ross, "Bin Laden's 'War of A Thousand Cuts' Will Live On," *The Atlantic*, May 3, 2011, online at www.theatlantic.com.

28   Marc A. Thiessen, "Bin Laden's Secret Plan to Destroy America: Make Joe Biden President," *American Enterprise Institute*, November 26, 2012, online at www.aei.org.

29   Joh Lee Anderson, "The Assassins," *The New Yorker*, June 10, 2022, p. 72.

30   See Mozhdah 2002, p. 85.

31   Zalmay Khalilzad, *The Envoy: From Kabul to the White House. My Journey Through a Turbulent World*, St. Martin's Press, 2016, p. 136.

32   Dam 2014, p. 169.

33   Woodward 2002, p. 81.

34   Woodward 2002, p. 81.

35   Mark Phelps, "Hijackers trained at U.S. flight schools," *AIN Online*, October 8, 2007, online at www.ainonline.com.

36   *The Guardian*, "Bush rejects Taliban offer to hand Bin Laden over," October 14, 2001, online at www.theguardian.com.

37   Jeremy Scahill, "The Nation: Blackwater: CIA Assassins?," *NPR*, August 24, 2009, online at www.npr.org.

38   Barbara Lee, *Renegade for Peace and Justice: A Memoir of Political and Personal Courage*, Rowman & Littlefield, 2011, p. 211.

39   Gerhard Schröder, "Erklärung der Bundesregierung zu den Anschlägen in den Vereinigten Staaten von Amerika," September 12, 2001, online at dserver.bundestag.de.

40   Gerhard Schröder, "Rede des Bundeskanzlers vor dem Bundestag anlässlich der Abstimmung über den Einsatz bewaffneter deutscher Streitkräfte im Kampf gegen den Terrorismus," November 16, 2001, online at dserver.bundestag.de.

41   Peter Struck, "Rede des Bundesministers der Verteidigung," Dezember 20, 2002, online at www.bundesregierung.de.

42   Tweet by Karim El-Gawhary, July 1, 2021, online at twitter.com.

43   George Packer, "How Rumsfeld Deserves to Be Remembered," *The Atlantic*, July 1, 2021, online at www.theatlantic.com.

44   Tweet by Jeremy Scahill, June 30, 2021, online at twitter.com.

45   Woodward 2002, p. 173.

46   Leandro Despouy et al., "Civil and political rights, including the questions of independence of the judiciary, administration of justice, impunity," September 12, 2006, p. 7, online at digitallibrary.un.org; see Human Rights Watch, "Creating Enemies of the State: Religious Persecution in Uzbekistan," 2004, online at www.hrw.org.

47   Craig Murray, "Why the US won't admit it was jilted," *The Guardian*, August 3, 2005, online at www.theguardian.com.

48   BBC, "Imran Khan criticized after calling Osama Bin Laden a 'martyr'," June 26, 2020, online at www.bbc.com.

49   Samuel P. Huntington, "The Clash of Civilizations?," summer 1993, online at www.foreignaffairs.com.

50   Amartya Sen, *Identity and Violence: The Illusion of Destiny*, W.W. Norton, 2007.

51   Pankaj Mishra, "Seit Beginn der Moderne erleben wir eine Krise der Männlichkeit," *Telepolis*, April 9, 2018, online at www.telepolis.de.

52   Joachim Hoelzgen, "Heiliger Krieg in Malakand: Angriff der Ur-Taliban," *Spiegel*, January 15, 2007, online at www.spiegel.de.

53   Winston S. Churchill, *The Story of the Malakand Field Force: An Episode of Frontier War*, 1898, online at www.gutenberg.org.

54   Priyamvada Gopal, "Why can't Britain handle the truth about Winston Churchill?," *The Guardian*, March 17, 2021, online at www.theguardian.com.

55   Shashi Tharoor, *Inglorious Empire: What the British Did to India*, Penguin, 2016, pp. 165ff.

56   Theodor Fontane, *Gesammelte Werke*, F. Fontane & Co, 1905, pp. 193ff.

57   Farrukh Husain, "A critical review of William Dalrymple's 'Return of a King,'" *The Frontier Post*, September 17, 2020, online at thefrontierpost.com.

58   Vincent Bevins, *The Jakarta Method: Washington's Anticommunist Crusade and the Mass Murder Program that Shaped Our World*, Public Affairs, 2020.

59   M. Hassan Kakar, *Afghanistan: The Soviet Invasion and the Afghan Response, 1979–1982*, University of California Press, 1995.

60   Christopher Andrew and Vasili Mitrokhin, *The World Was Going Our Way: The KGB and the Battle for the Third World*, Basic Books, 2006.

61   The complete UN report from 1986 can be found at https://www.refworld.org/docid/482996d02.html.

62   Michael Bérubé, *The Left at War*, NYU Press, 2009, p. 261.

63   Emran Feroz, Interview with KHAD agent speaking on
condition of anonymity, April 2021.

64   Conor Tobin, "The Myth of the 'Afghan Trap': Zbigniew
Brzezinski and Afghanistan, 1978–1979," *Diplomatic History*,
vol. 44, April 2020, pp. 237–264.

65   Wesley Morgan, *The Hardest Place: The American Military
Adrift in Afghanistan's Pech Valley*, Random House, 2021.

66   Amnesty International, "Mapping CIA Black Sites," April 5,
2010, online at www.amnestyusa.org.

67   Ulrike Demmer et al., "Rekonstruktion vom Kunduz-
Anschlag: Ein deutsches Verbrechen," *Spiegel*, October 6,
2016, online at www.spiegel.de.

68   *Frankfurter Allgemeine Zeitung*, "Kundus-Bombardement:
Kein Disziplinarverfahren gegen Oberst Klein," August 19,
2010, online at www.faz.net.

69   *Augen geradeaus*, "Bonner Landgericht: Keine
Amtspflichtverletzung von Oberst Klein bei Kundus-
Luftangriff", December 11, 2013, online at
www.augengeradeaus.net.

70   Rory Callinan, "Photo reveals Australian soldier drinking beer
out of dead Taliban fighter's prosthetic leg," *The Guardian*,
December 1, 2020, online at www.theguardian.com.

71   The Afghanistan Inquiry Report, the official report on the war
crimes of the SAS in Afghanistan from November 2020, can
be found online at www.defence.gov.au.

72   Nick McKenzie, Joel Tozer, and Chris Masters, "Killings
of Afghans 'happened all the time,'" *The Age*, November 15,
2020, online at www.theage.com.au.

73   John Lyons. "AFP raid on ABC reveals investigative
journalism being put in same category as criminality," ABC,
July 15, 2019, online at www.abc.net.

74   Ali M Latifi, "Afghans recall days when Australians unleashed dogs, gunfire," November 19, 2020, online at: www.aljazeera.com.

75   Author interview with Bilal Sarwary, June 2021.

76   Mark Willacy, "'They decided to kill all of them,'" ABC, June 8, 2021, online at www.abc.net.

77   Samantha Maiden, "Samantha Crompvoets hit with legal demand to prove book doesn't pose 'national security' risk," *news.com.au*, June 8, 2021, online at news.com.au.

78   Murray Brewster, "The fall of Panjwaii casts a long shadow over Canada's Afghan war veterans," *CBC*, July 10, 2021, online at www.cbc.ca.

79   Richard Luscombe, "Navy Seal pardoned of war crimes by Trump described by colleagues as 'freaking evil,'" *The Guardian*, December 27, 2019, online at www.theguardian.com.

80   Rachel E. Van Landingham and Geoffrey S. Corn, "Trump's Blackwater pardons erase the line between slaughter and justified wartime violence," *USA Today*, December 23, 2020, online at www.usatoday.com.

81   David "Bull" Gurfein, "President Trump Must Act on Behalf of Robert Bales and Other Convicted Warfighters," January 4, 2021, online at www.military.com.

82   Habib Zahori, "Tales of 'White Taliban' Sketch a New Legend," July 23, 2013, online at www.atwar.blogs.nytimes.com.

83   Author interview with Erik Edstrom, November 2020.

84   Erik Edstrom, *Un-American: A Soldier's Reckoning of Our Longest War*, Bloomsbury, 2020, p. 2.

85   WDR Monitor, "Bundeswehr verschweigt zivile Opfer bei Afghanistan-Offensive," *WDR*, July 10, 2014, online at presse.wdr.de.

86 *Bild*, "Auf geheimer Mission mit dem KSK: Jagd auf den Mörder eines Kameraden in Afghanistan," April 28, 2020, online at www.youtube.com.

87 Sebastian Erb, "Rechtsextremismus beim KSK: Mit Reformen ist es nicht getan," June 15, 2021, online at www.taz.de.

88 Amnesty International, "Mapping CIA Black Sites," April 5, 2010, online at www.amnestyusa.org.

89 Ruslan Trad, "The Soviet Origins of Putin's Mercenaries," April 27, 2021, online at newlinesmag.com.

90 Author interview with Mohamedou Ould Slahi, January 2021.

91 Human Rights Watch, "Mauritania: Allow Ex-Guantanamo Detainee to Travel," June 13, 2019, online at www.hrw.org.

92 The *New York Times*, "The Guantanamo Docket," June 17, 2021, online at www.nytimes.com.

93 *The Afghan Eye Podcast*, episode from July 13, 2020, online at https://www.facebook.com/afgeyeFB/

94 Raniah Salloum, "Anführer des 'Islamischen Staats': Die Knastbrüder von Camp Bucca," November 5, 2014, online at www.spiegel.de; Christoph Reuter, "Neuer IS-Chef al-Salbi Baghdadis Erbe," January 22, 2020, online at www.spiegel.de.

95 Emran Feroz, "'Islamischer Staat' versus 'Taliban-Emirat': Ein Kalif zu viel," February 18, 2015, online at de.qantara.de.

96 BBC, "American Sniper film 'behind rise in anti-Muslim threats,'" January 25, 2015, online at www.bbc.com.

97 Robert Johnson, "The Pork Eating Crusader Patch Is a Huge Hit With Troops In Afghanistan," March 17, 2012, online at www.businessinsider.com.

98   Matthias Gebauer, "Afghanistans Präsident Karzai Steinmeier besucht den Problem-Partner," February 9, 2014, online at www.spiegel.de.

99   Jonathan Steele and Jon Boone, "WikiLeaks: Afghan vice-president 'landed in Dubai with $52m in cash,'" December 2, 2010, online at www.theguardian.com.

100 Jessica Purkiss, "The Afghan officials' families with luxury pads in Dubai," November 4, 2019, online at www.thebureauinvestigates.com.

101 Julia Maria Amberger, "Gekaufte Freundschaft," June 13, 2013, online at www.taz.de.

102 Dam 2014, p. 14; Jeff Stein, "CIA Honors Officer Who Saved Karzai's Life," September 18, 2017, online at www.newsweek.com.

103 James Risen, "Reports Link Karzai's Brother to Afghanistan Heroin Trade," October 4, 2008, online at www.nytimes.com; Alfred Mccoy, *In the Shadows of the American Century: The Rise and Decline of US Global Power*, Haymarket Books, 2017, p. 67.

104 Al Jazeera America, "High turnout in Afghanistan elections," April 5, 2014, online at america.aljazeera.com.

105 Emran Feroz, *Tod per Knopfdruck: Das wahre Ausmaß des US-Drohnen-Terrors oder Wie Mord zum Alltag werden konnte*, Westend, 2017.

106 Jack Serle, "If drone strikes continue in Afghanistan, the lack of transparency must not," October 16, 2014, online at www.thebureauinvestigates.com.

107 Feroz 2017, pp. 167ff.

108 May Jeong, "Losing Sight: A 4-Year-Old Girl Was the Sole Survivor of a U.S. Drone Strike in Afghanistan. Then She Disappeared," January 27, 2018, online at www.theintercept.com.

109 Oriana Pawlyk, "The US conducted more airstrikes in Afghanistan in 2018 than any other time in the last decade," February 12, 2019, online at www.taskandpurpose.com; Julian Borger, "US dropped record number of bombs on Afghanistan last year," January 28, 2020, online at www.theguardian.com.

110 Murray Jones, "40% of all civilian casualties from airstrikes in Afghanistan—almost 1,600—in the last five years were children," May 6, 2021, online at https://aoav.org.uk.

111 Jessica Purkiss, "The families paying the price for the war in Afghanistan," June 3, 2020, online at www.thebureauinvestigates.com.

112 Ehsan Qaane, "Afghan War Crimes Trials in The Netherlands: Who are the suspects and what have been the outcomes?" March 25, 2020, online at www.afghanistan-analysts.org.

113 CBC News, "Afghan governor's rights abuses known in '07," April 12, 2010, online at www.cbc.ca.

114 Emran Feroz, "Atrocities Pile Up for CIA-Backed Afghan Paramilitary Forces," November 16 2020, online at www.foreignpolicy.com.

115 BBC, "BBC reporter Ahmad Shah killed in Afghanistan attack," April 30, 2018, online at www.bbc.com.

116 Clemens Neuhold, "Solche jungen Afghanen kommen bereits kriminell nach Österreich," *Profil*, July 02, 2021, online at www.profil.at.

117 BBC News, "'No sympathy for Afghan migrants': President Ashraf Ghani," March 31, 2016, online at www.youtube.com.

118 Kate Martyr, "George W. Bush: Afghanistan troop withdrawal 'a mistake,'" July 14, 2021, online at www.dw.com.

119 Azmat Khan, "Ghost Students, Ghost Teachers, Ghost Schools," July 9, 2015, online at www.buzzfeednews.com.

120 Hijatullah Darwazi, "See the real face of Fawzia Koofi and her corrupt family!," December 6, 2015, online at www.rawa.org; Thomas Ruttig, "Eldorado am Hindukusch: Krieg und Kriegsgewinnler in Afghanistan," November 24, 2018, online at thruttig.wordpress.com.

121 See the website of Gharnata, www.gharnata.net.

122 Author interviews with Abdul Kadir Mohmand, 2019–2021.

123 Author interview with Saidal Mohmand, June 2021.

124 Wesley Morgan, "Our secret Taliban air force," October 22, 2020, online at www.washingtonpost.com.

125 Julian Borger, "Trump reportedly tells Taliban official 'you are a tough people' in first phone call," March 3, 2020, online at www.theguardian.com.

126 Craig Whitlock, "At War with the Truth," The *Washington Post*, December 19, 2019, online at www.washingtonpost.com

127 John Sopko, "Setting the record straight on 'The Afghanistan Papers,'" December 17, 2019, online at www.washingtonpost.com.

128 Emran Feroz, "In Afghanistan, the freedoms of the press are under attack," December 18, 2020, *Columbia Journalism Review*, online at www.cjr.org.

129 UN Report, "Protection of Civilians in Armed Conflict 2021 Quarterly Report," April 14, 2021, online at unama.unmissions.org.

130 Morgan 2021, p. 32.